NO BOOK BEGINNERS

A STEP-BY-STEP FRAMEWORK FOR CREATIVE
PIANO TEACHING, RIGHT FROM LESSON ONE

TIM TOPHAM

Text copyright © 2023 by Top Music Education PTY LTD

All rights reserved.

No part of this book may be reproduced, or stored in a retrieval system, or transmitted in any form or by any means, electronic, mechanical, photocopying, recording, or otherwise, without express written permission of the publisher.

Published by Top Music Education PTY LTD, Melbourne, Australia

topmusic.co

ISBN-13: 978-0-6486051-1-9 (paperback)

Cover design by © Aldren Gamalo / 99designs.com.au

Cover illustration by © rawpixel.com / freepik.com

Interior design by Kelly Exeter

To my first piano teacher, Ms Rosemary Rhodes (Miss Mac) — I may never have taken a musical path in life without your influence.

Contents

Foreword 1
Introduction 5
   No Book Beginners (NBB) Is Born 9
   Is NBB for You? 14
   A Little Bit About Me 15
   About This Book 16

Part 1: How We Got Here and Why Change Is Needed . 19
   A Little Bit of History 24
   Why Is Teaching Reading Such a Big Thing Today? 26
   If I'm Not Teaching Reading, What Is There to Do? 30
   What If I Took Your Method Books Away? 31
   Technical Deficiencies That May Arise from
   Method-Book Teaching 32
   Beginner Boredom Can Be Terminal 35
   Self-Assessment 1: Teaching Beginners 37
   Reconsidering the Reading-First Approach to
   Learning Piano 42
   Takeaways 43

Part 2: Three Foundational Mindsets for Change . . . 45
   1. A More Holistic Approach to Music Teaching 50
   2. Student-Centred Teaching 52

Self-Assessment 2: How Student Centred is Your
Teaching Right Now? 55

3. A More Creative Approach 60

Self-Assessment 3: How Creative Are Your Current
Piano Lessons? 66

What If I'm Not Creative? 71

Is It OK to Spend Time on All This Creativity? 74

The Benefits of a Creative Approach to Music Teaching . 76

Getting Parents on Board with the Creative Approach . . 78

Takeaways 79

Part 3: The NBB Framework and Lesson Plans 81

Common Questions I Get Asked About the Framework . . 84

Core Fundamentals 89

The NBB Lesson Plans 95

My Beginner Teaching Goals 96

Lesson 1 100

Lesson 2 108

Lesson 3 115

Lesson 4 120

Lesson 5 123

Lesson 6 128

Lesson 7 129
Lesson 8 129
Lesson 9 130
Lesson 10 130
Beyond Lesson 10. 131
The NBB Benefits. 132
Takeaways. 140

Part 4: Atypical Beginners. 141
Preschoolers 143
Teens and Adults 149
Transfer Students 151
Neurodiverse Students and those with Exceptionalities . . 152
Takeaways. 156

Conclusion 157
Epilogue 161
Resources 165
Social Media Links 169
20 Creative Ways to Start a Piano Lesson 171
Acknowledgements 175
About the Author 181
Endnotes 183

Foreword

BY PHILIP JOHNSTON

In 1968 at the Mexico Summer Olympics, an American high jumper won a gold medal using a technique that to spectators seemed absurd, and to traditionalists, heretical. The loping, curved run up and backwards flop looked nothing like the high jumping that had gone before; it proved not only to be a viable alternative but a template for a better way. It's fitting that the technique has been named for the athlete who pioneered it, with the Fosbury flop being used by every gold medal-winning high jumper since.

This book's central idea has the potential to revolutionise early piano teaching just like the Fosbury flop revolutionised the high jump. The question it poses will to many parents seem absurd, to teachers heretical: What might be possible when a piano student's early lessons are no longer all about learning to read?

What fresh goals, early steps, success touchstones and neglected skills are recast when a student's focus is redirected to the keyboard instead of the music stand? How different might studio recitals be when the same old procession of 'Harold the Hippo Plays Middle C' (Book 1) is replaced by pieces students improvise, or compose, or play by ear, or play in ensemble, or add their own harmonies to, or explore with black-note-only pentatonic scales, or, or, or …

This is a book about those ors — countless, delicious, fertile, lesson-powering, music-stand-closed ors that give teachers a wealth of new options when the primer-based treadmill is failing to inspire.

Tim Topham is exactly the right advocate for this urgent and overdue reform. His podcasts alone are a formidable assembly of a who's who of international piano pedagogy expertise, his piano teacher online communities and in-person events abuzz with conversation and innovation. Anyone who knows Tim will know that this book was never going to be a cold, academic thesis; it's warm, replete with examples and idea-starters that trust the reader to build studios and systems of their own.

My wish for the book? That there is significant pushback — as in everyone-is-talking-about-this-and-it's-got-some-teachers-really-mad levels of pushback. The core

FOREWORD

proposition should be discussed white-hot wherever piano teachers gather. At stake is a return to piano as a medium for creation, rather than re-creation, and a vastly expanded tool kit of options for teachers and students alike. Kids won't take piano lessons; they'll explore piano. And in time — make no mistake — they will dazzle us with what they've been freed to create.

— Philip Johnston

Introduction

Have you ever read something or heard a speech that upended all your preconceived ideas about a topic?

This happened to me in 2015 when I was attending my first National Conference on Keyboard Pedagogy (NCKP) in Chicago. One of the presentations there had ramifications for my teaching that persist through to today. Indeed, the profound impact it had on my pedagogical thinking is core to everything I share in this book.

At that NCKP conference, one of the keynote speakers, Dr Edwin Gordon, was unable to speak due to illness. Little did we all know at the time that Dr Gordon's illness would persist. He sadly passed away later the same year. While I'd not heard of Dr Gordon, other attendees certainly knew who he was and couldn't wait to hear what he had to say. Dr Scott Price, head of the conference, had this to say about Dr Gordon's absence:

> *He is a true legend in the field of music education, and the full impact of his work is only beginning to be felt in the piano teaching community. We are very saddened that Dr Gordon's health prevents him from being with us at this time but are heartened that he has asked us to have his keynote address read at the conference. While nothing can replace his presence at our event, we're pleased that we will have him with us in thoughts and words.[1]*

Dr Price then proceeded to read out Dr Gordon's keynote speech, and I was mesmerised. One of Dr Gordon's early statements had me nodding vigorously because it affirmed everything I knew about the music teaching landscape. Indeed, it was a reality of instrumental music teaching that I had been trying to change for five years:

> *I am led to believe the piano is taught to many persons by teachers who typically teach the way they were taught rather than according to an objective learning theory and current research.[2]*

The speech went on to outline the research behind Dr Gordon's *Music Learning Theory* (MLT) and the discovery he'd made that the best way to introduce children to music is *not through the traditional avenue of method books*. Rather, it is the same way you'd teach a language: through experience and imitation — before reading and writing.

INTRODUCTION

Exposure to this thought and Dr Gordon's MLT method triggered something in me.

As a pianist, I was really good at improvising and jamming with other musicians. I could play lots of instruments and I did lots of accompanying. But when I started teaching, like many first-time teachers, I fell back to what I knew: teaching the way my own teacher had taught me.

The problem was the old paradigm of focusing music education on reading, performance and interpretation *was clearly not working* for the majority of students today.

In later years, whenever I would take on a transfer student or run a mock exam for another teacher, I was constantly baffled by the fact that many students could play well but struggled with simple musicality skills like singing, playing by ear, discriminating pitch and repeating rhythmic patterns. Or they'd be happily playing in 3/4 time and add or remove a beat from the measure without noticing.

If I asked them to 'just play something in C major', they had no idea what to do. If I asked them to make up a melody over my accompaniment, they stared back in bewilderment. Their aural skills were poor — if I could get them to even sing at all! — and their general knowledge of music was severely lacking. And I knew these things weren't just limited to the students I was interacting with; I saw the same observations mentioned time and again by fellow teachers in online discussions.

The conference also made me realise that there were things I was confident doing myself but wasn't teaching to students. The traditional reading approach seemed to be contributing to this.

So, when I returned from NCKP, I went deep with my research about getting the best out of teaching beginners — really deep!

- ♪ I interviewed professors and authors who'd had the most success in teaching beginners and found out their best tricks.
- ♪ I went to masterclasses and lectures about music learning.
- ♪ I interviewed specialists in Kodály, Orff, Suzuki and MLT.
- ♪ I read and learnt as much about MLT as I could.[3]

While the MLT method resonated most deeply with me, I continued to run into one challenge: I couldn't find an MLT *beginner* method I was comfortable using.[4] So I began trying out lots of different ideas discovered during my research, borrowing activities from multiple teaching approaches and testing them on all my beginner students. I got them chanting, singing, clapping, tapping, using percussion, getting off the bench and playing games. You name it, I tried it. It clearly made sense for more time

INTRODUCTION

to be spent on listening, singing, moving and clapping than on reading at the start. It also aligned with my own understanding of how I play and experience music.

Then the breakthrough happened.

Late in 2015, I began working with a new beginner student, Josh, who was a fun, outgoing seven-year-old, madly into Australian Rules football, skiing ... and music! With all my research in hand and preliminary testing done, I committed myself to teaching Josh for one term (a ten-week teaching block in Australia) *completely without method books*. Yes, no books at all for ten weeks. And the short story is ... it was a success! Such a success, in fact, that it set me on the path of documenting my own approach for other teachers to use.

No Book Beginners (NBB) Is Born

One of the biggest challenges I've faced over the years is implementing the teaching ideas I was learning about from books, lectures and workshops. I found that unless you had one-on-one teaching from a master, it was often really hard to understand what to do.

So, when I began developing my ten-week program of 'no book' creative piano lessons, my main goal was that it could easily be implemented by regular teachers accustomed to method books. When it came time to share my approach with the world, I was apprehensive: *Would it work for teachers who weren't me?* The apprehension evaporated quickly as success stories started to pour in. Many were from teachers who were classically trained, nervous about trying something different and only doing so because nothing else was working.

Take Valerie, whose shy student wouldn't do anything in her lesson at first until she opened up with some ideas from the NBB approach:

> *I had a student who came in with her mum and big sister. She was shy and refused to look at me, talk to me, or play anything — until I showed her some improv ideas about the Fourth of July and fireworks (which we were getting ready to celebrate the next day). All of a sudden, she started asking if she could show me a song she knew before playing 'Hot Cross Buns'. I springboarded from there and played 'Mary Had a Little Lamb'. The next song she wanted to show me was a very rough version of 'Für Elise' — just a few of the first notes, but I figured out quickly what she was playing and played just the beginning right-hand theme with two hands. Her eyes got very wide, and her first smile appeared! After that, we started black key improv, and she said she already knew the names of the white keys and could start from the highest key and named each one going backwards! I praised her for how much she already*

INTRODUCTION

knew and encouraged her with some ideas for C–D–E improv. She was counting groups of two and three black keys and finding every C before the lesson ended.

Sarah, a music teacher at a school, had one of her piano students run up to her in the yard and share his excitement with her:

My Thursday eight-year-old had a great time. He came rushing up to me at recess at school to tell me about his Egyptian music. I took a video in the lesson and was so proud of him. He chatted all the way through: 'This is the snake, and he's even a dangerous snake.' He made up the words here and there, which he chanted in rhythm. He told me, 'This is the really scary part.' He reused motives in logical ways. Wow![5] *The most surprising thing was when he told me that he didn't do much practice from the tutor book because he was too busy making up his song. I replied, 'That's fantastic progress — there's plenty of time for that later!'*

Timothy had a story for those with students who struggle to find the motivation to practise:

I've loved your NBB approach, which I've been using to teach a second-grade boy. We are going to be doing our fourth lesson this week. What's great is that he's really enjoying it, and apparently he practises a lot without needing anyone to tell him to.

Another downside of some beginner programs I've explored over the years is that they are often *too* prescriptive and lock teachers into a very strict regime with little opportunity for deviating from their approach. Some trademarked programs even ban it under the terms of their licences! I wasn't happy with that. I wanted to be able to do my own thing! And I wanted to keep things simple and clear.

Indeed, criticism was even levelled at music learning theory itself that speaks to this challenge. Paul G. Woodford states in his article that 'Gordon's system is too prescriptive and proscriptive to students and teachers, and that music educators should also be aware of the diversity of practices [available].'[6]

This is why, when developing NBB, I knew I wanted it to be a *framework* rather than a *method*. I designed it to be something on which to scaffold your teaching and provide ideas and direction — something to work *alongside* your current teaching style, or even just something to try as a replacement for a single student. As you read through this book, I want to emphasise that *how* you use this approach is totally up to you. I encourage you to explore, remix and edit it as much as you wish. I'm not precious about how

INTRODUCTION

my ideas are used and you'll need to adapt them to suit each student in any case!

Many teachers are pretty confident playing lead sheets and improvising simple melodies — perhaps for church or playing for musicals. But what most teachers are lacking is a *systematic framework for teaching those skills to students*. That's exactly what the NBB framework provides, because I know it can be really hard to break down how to teach things that you're already very good at.

Later in this book, I will share the first five NBB lessons, and you will see they provide guidelines for:

- ♪ the basics of technique, sitting position and knowledge of the keyboard
- ♪ immersing students in creative music-making activities that will hopefully continue for a lifetime
- ♪ challenging students to explore music and be curious about how it works
- ♪ the fundamentals of metre, rhythm, beat and time and how they feel in their bodies
- ♪ helping students transpose tunes and hear and understand harmony
- ♪ helping students listen, sing and pitch-match from the beginning

- ♪ helping students be 100% engaged and having fun with music before they start the next phase: reading.

Is NBB for You?

This book is for:

- ♪ independent music teachers who feel there might be a better way of teaching beginners but are not sure what that looks like
- ♪ teachers who've sometimes questioned whether all the music reading from the start is the right way
- ♪ teachers who perhaps haven't experienced a lot of training and would like more confidence in their approach
- ♪ classically trained teachers who find it hard to break from the way they were taught and try new, creative ideas in lessons
- ♪ teachers who find students hard to connect with, inspire and motivate amongst the distractions of today (sports, technology, dance, drama)
- ♪ teachers wondering why the approach they've used for years is no longer working as well as it used to and why students are dropping off from lessons

INTRODUCTION

♪ teachers who already teach creatively but haven't had a structure or framework around it and who sometimes feel they might be teaching students the 'wrong way'.

This book is designed to inspire *you* to not only try more creativity in your lessons but to come up with your own creative 'no book' ideas. I believe that you can do amazing things with only a few ideas to spark your imagination and the confidence to give it a shot.

The framework is designed for teaching beginner piano students around six to ten years old, having 30- to 45-minute weekly lessons. While it is aimed primarily at teachers working one-on-one with students in a private studio, it has been successfully adapted for classroom and group settings by many teachers.

A Little Bit About Me

I've spent more than 20 years teaching in Australia and internationally as a classroom teacher, private studio teacher, head of department and head of campus. I've taught and coordinated subjects including outdoor education, mathematics, information technology and, of course, music! Over the past 13 years, I've become recognised as an international leader in music education, and this has seen me speak on stages all around the world, from the US to the UK and Australia, about a more creative, modern and integrated approach to music teaching.

I *passionately* believe in a holistic approach to teaching music that resonates with young people and inspires them to continue playing well into adulthood.

About This Book

This book is based on an amalgam of my writings, as far back as 2010. It represents knowledge I've assimilated from:

- ♪ interviewing over 300 podcast guests
- ♪ writing more than 150 articles for magazines and blog posts
- ♪ testing countless teaching ideas, methods, and approaches
- ♪ attending and participating in hundreds of masterclasses, workshops, and events
- ♪ attaining my own performance diploma through lessons with my teacher, concert pianist Caroline Almonte
- ♪ attending and speaking at international conventions
- ♪ helping teachers across the world for 13 years both individually and in groups.

INTRODUCTION

It's been immensely rewarding to put this book together. I enjoyed going back over blog posts and articles I'd written right back to 2010 when timtopham.com (as it was then known) was established. I've reread the transcripts of countless podcast interviews, rewatched videos from my first (embarrassing) YouTube efforts (yes, they're still on my channel if you want to watch!) and did even more research on how things have changed in the almost ten years since my experience at NCKP.

I really enjoyed diving into the writing and work of the late Forrest Kinney, one of our TopMusicPro[7] expert teachers and another pioneer in creative piano teaching. I rewatched our webinars, interviews and the course he created for us. I particularly appreciated reading his extended essays about why music has moved so far away from creativity over the last 200 years. You'll see some of his writing and thoughts referenced throughout this text.

Over the journey of this book, I will share:

- ♪ how we got to this place where method books are the basis of most beginner piano lessons
- ♪ the problems this has created and why changes are needed to address those problems
- ♪ what those changes look like

- ♫ what 'creative' music teaching looks like and how you can gain confidence teaching creatively
- ♫ the underlying principles of the NBB framework
- ♫ the full lesson plans for the first five NBB lessons
- ♫ the benefits of using the NBB approach
- ♫ how to manage atypical beginners — preschoolers, teenagers, adults and students with additional needs.

This book is a condensed version of all the most important information you need to understand the thinking behind the NBB approach. If you want to read more about any of the ideas shared here and to access additional free resources, just head to our companion website nobookbeginners.com to explore topics of particular interest further.

PART 1

How We Got Here and Why Change is Needed

'Dad! Dad! Look what I made!' My son Jack came bursting through the door after school, eager to show me something in his bag. 'We did this cool thing in art, and I brought it home for you,' he said as he dumped his bag in the kitchen and started rummaging through it, eager to find his creation.

'Awesome! Do you want something to eat?' I asked as I headed for the pantry.

'Maybe later,' he replied without thinking.

Jack's your typical Year 4 kid — forever bringing things home from school. Normally, those things end up in a scrunched mess at the bottom of his bag smeared in banana and smelling like an old sock, so I was pleasantly surprised when this one appeared in one piece.

'Wow, Jack, that's so cool! What is it?'

He held out his creation to me. It was a small pottery cup, painted in a variety of colours and hanging from three pieces of string tied through holes near the rim of the cup and joined at the top, a bit like a marionette.

As it spun around, I noted a face drawn in texta on one side and pipe cleaners (chenille stems) sticking out through holes around the face. Some of the pipe cleaners were adorned with beads near the ends and were all different colours.

'Come to think of it,' I thought aloud, 'it looks a little like SpongeBob SquarePants!'

'It's a cup person, silly,' he replied.

'Oh, of course. Now I see the face and the arms and legs. Wow, Jack, this is fantastic!'

'Yeah, his name's Bob, and he can hang around and watch what you do. See?' He held the top of the strings where the three pieces connected and hung it over a cupboard handle with the face pointing towards us. Bob slowly spun around in the light.

Despite how his creation looked, the excitement on my son's face filled me with pride, and I knew he'd enjoy showing others his wacky creation when they would visit the house.

I laughed. 'Nice one. We should find a place to keep him safe so that everyone who comes to the house can check him out.'

'Yeah sure,' he replied. And then he was off — other exciting things to do. 'Can Billy come over?' he shouted as he ran upstairs to change. And with that, the moment was gone.

But not for me. As a music teacher with more than 20 years of experience, I found myself pondering, *Why don't students learning music get to bring home their own creations, just like they do in art?* I started thinking back to all the other things our boys had brought home from school over the years: paintings, etchings, carvings, fluffy balls, papier mâché, models and more.

And then I started thinking back to my own school art classes and all the trinkets and knick-knacks I created and excitedly shared with my own parents. In my childhood home, we had a wide picture rail running the length of the hallway filled with homemade pottery boxes, medieval drinking cups, vases and, of course back in those days, ashtrays, made by my siblings and me. I remember how proudly they'd be on display at home and remain there for years, even as we grew older. The thought of throwing them out was considered sacrilegious in some way.

When my thoughts returned to the present, I felt a sense of loss for:

- ♪ all the missed opportunities for music students to create something on their instrument and bring it home for their families to enjoy
- ♪ all the musicians who enjoyed composing but were never encouraged or nurtured in their pursuit
- ♪ all the music students who'd never enjoy the sense of satisfaction that comes with creating something personal, from scratch, that is their own
- ♪ the parents who never experienced the joy of their children's musical creations, no matter how simple or discordant.

I began to wonder … *Why **don't** we give opportunities for kids to create things to take home in music lessons, just like they've always done in art class? Why hasn't Jack ever brought home wacky little creations from his music lessons? Why isn't music **creation** a regular part of the music lesson experience?*

A Little Bit of History

The norm for any student when they start piano lessons, is to be taught via a method book and the majority of teachers will use them right from lesson one. There are many reasons why this has become commonplace.

HOW WE GOT HERE AND WHY CHANGE IS NEEDED

Method books:

- ♪ are well designed
- ♪ are easy to follow
- ♪ build knowledge in a logical sequence
- ♪ are what we know best
- ♪ don't require a lot of thinking or planning on behalf of the teacher.

But they're all designed for one main purpose — to teach music *reading*. Sure, they cover aspects of artistry and interpretation. But by and large, their purpose is the teaching and deciphering of printed scores so that students can become more and more proficient in this area and play increasingly more complex music.

While there's nothing wrong with teaching music reading per se, we have to ask ourselves, *Is that the most important part of being a musician?* And perhaps more importantly, given the focus of this book, *Is that the best thing to teach students right from the start?*

I would argue a definitive *no*. This book will explain why that's my stance and share what to do instead.

But before we get there, let's explore why method books and reading have become such a prevalent part of early music education.

Why Is Teaching Reading Such a Big Thing Today?

Music lessons weren't always like they are now.

In the early 1700s (around the time of Johann Sebastian Bach), if you couldn't improvise, you couldn't work as a musician. The main employment opportunities back then were court-appointed roles in which the musician's job was to make music for various events, festivities, church services and pageants. In short, musicians of the time had to be great at *creating* music. So it should come as no surprise that this is when Handel created his *Music for the Royal Fireworks* and *Water Music*, when Bach wrote the *Brandenburg Concertos*, and when Pachelbel decided that the key of D was perfect for a canon.

What did life for piano students look like in those days? Lucinda Mackworth-Young, my guest on TopMusic Podcast Episode 110, shared:

> *If we go back to the 'olden days', people were learning to play instruments before printed music was widely available (and thus very, very expensive). In the very early days of the keyboard, you would have been taught by just preluding on chords. Then you would be improvising. Then maybe you'd learn to read a little bit of music as*

> *well, but it would be a very holistic thing. Since the advent of unbelievably prevalent sheet music, we've become very tied to the written note. That also was because many composers would get upset if you weren't playing precisely what they wanted you to play.* [8]

Acclaimed marketer Seth Godin agrees. In a presentation he gave to final-year performance students at Carnegie Mellon University, he explained that, prior to audio recording, performing the works of the masters was an important art. But that quickly changed.

> *Playing it as written was critical in 1920 because fidelity was the goal. These people are only going to hear this symphony once; play it as written. That is what the composer earned — the privilege of having you play it as written. And in 1890, play it as written. But today, a company called Naxos has virtually every symphony you could ever want, and if you want it on CD, it's only $5; if you want it online, it's free. So the value component (of performing old works as written) just fell away. The number of [performances] I need of a given symphony played as written is now zero. I don't need any more. If no one made a particular [performance] of a given symphony, no one would miss it.* [9]

NO BOOK BEGINNERS

In the Classical era, Mozart and Beethoven were still playing their own compositions and riffing on popular themes of the time. But, as Forrest Kinney noted:

> *In the latter part of Beethoven's life, printed masterworks by him, Bach, and many others became widely available for the first time. Within a generation, pianists began to see themselves as akin to Shakespearean actors, performers with the noble purpose of bringing to life the profound musical scripts of the masters. Pedagogy followed, conservatories were born, and to this day, many (if not most) music students are taught to recite and perform the works of others but not to improvise, arrange, or compose themselves.*[10]

Once sheet music publishing became popular in the early to mid-1800s, it had a huge effect on the world of music.

We might call this the beginning of the 'era of music publishing', though it's useful to note that in the 1850s there still wasn't a way to play back prerecorded music. Instead, it was the intellectual property of the composition that formed the backbone of music publishing law as we understand it. As musical performances of existing works began to take on greater importance in the music halls, dance clubs and theatres of Europe and the United States, the demand for sheet music of popular works only grew.[11]

HOW WE GOT HERE AND WHY CHANGE IS NEEDED

With recorded music being some way off (the phonograph only truly hit the mass market after 1910) and the advent of sheet music making it easier to find music from masters like Beethoven, Bach and Handel, musicians were encouraged to reproduce the written music as authentically as possible. This meant that the central focus of piano pedagogy turned towards converting students into *performers*, not *creators*. This is why, when you compare music to any of the other creative arts of the time — sculpture, painting and writing — music stands alone. Musicians are rarely (even to this day) encouraged to *create* music in the same way a painter would be encouraged to paint a new picture. Where an artist reproducing a painting by another painter would be considered a forger, this is not the case in music. Forrest Kinney says:

> *After printed music literature first became widely available in the 19th century, pianists were trained to be solo performers of the scores of Bach, Beethoven and others. I call this the Performer Model. Most of us were trained according to this model.*[12]

Method books emerged rapidly in the early 1900s when the piano became more popular and affordable in homes. Doreen Hall says:

> *The time period around 1925 is referred to as the 'Golden Age of the Piano'. The instrument gained popularity as many piano manufacturers made the purchase of a piano attainable for middle-class families. To coincide with the surge in interest, a 'New Age' of piano method was born. These newer piano books promised to make learning the piano more fun and featured whimsical songs and illustrations.*[13]

The advent of method books only sought to reinforce the idea that learning to play the piano was about learning to read and perform *other people's music*, which goes a long way to explaining the situation we find ourselves in today with such a focus on music reading.

If I'm Not Teaching Reading, What Is There to Do?

One of the disadvantages of music reading becoming the raison d'être for music education is that if a student doesn't want to learn to read music, most music teachers lose their sense of purpose and feel adrift. I've spoken to many teachers who feel this way and wonder, 'What can I teach them if I'm not teaching them to read?' Many teachers will even tell me that a student who doesn't want to learn to read has no place in their studio. What a sad outcome for the student!

Students need to learn to read eventually, and method books are a great, scaffolded approach to reading. But reading is only *part* of the musical experience and doesn't need to be the *first thing* students experience in lessons. There is so much more that teachers can bring to lessons than just reading. With all our years of performing and learning experience, teachers can help non-reading students with interpretation, articulation, dynamics and general musicality instead.

And it's often the case that students who don't want to read change their minds later on and want to be taught to read music. This has happened to me on a number of occasions.

What If I Took Your Method Books Away?

So what would you do if I took away your method books for the first five to ten lessons with a new student? How would you feel? What would you do?

Would you feel:

- ♪ liberated?
- ♪ terrified?
- ♪ embarrassed that you wouldn't really know what to do?

♪ excited about the possibilities of creating your own teaching program from scratch?

If you're like most classically trained teachers, you'd probably freak out a little, want the method book back, and hate me forever!

And given there are millions of kids learning piano around the world right now via method books — it's estimated that around 50 million kids worldwide are studying piano[14] — something must be working, right?

There are two main reasons why I feel change is needed:

1. Our current methods are creating technical challenges that hamper musical development.
2. Bored students are unlikely to continue with piano lessons and become lifelong musicians.

Technical Deficiencies That May Arise from Method-Book Teaching

Method books are great at teaching students to read and understand note values and pitch, but there are also some typical, suboptimal outcomes I see in students on a method book-only diet. Here are five of the most important. These outcomes are particularly prevalent in older methods — it's important to note that some newer methods are finally starting to include activities to mitigate some of these deficiencies.

1. Students Don't Like Singing and Have Poor Aural and Tonal Perception

Singing is a critical skill for all musicians but one that is often overlooked (or let's be honest, avoided) in traditional piano lessons. Singing allows students to engage with music more personally and deeply. It improves phrase shaping and is a critical skill for playing by ear.

Few methods encourage listening and singing right from the beginning. If singing isn't normalised at the start, it can be very difficult to encourage students to sing later on. Teachers can become really frustrated with students who won't make a sound when they need to take aural tests for exams. They wonder why they aren't able to pitch-match, discern intervals, clap back rhythms and so forth. It's primarily because these are not skills that were developed at the start.

2. Students Lack an Internal Sense of Beat and Metre

Oftentimes in the pursuit of reading, a student's internal sense of pulse is forgotten. This shows up in students adding an extra beat to a measure of 3/4 time, being unable to play along to a metronome or keep a steady beat themselves or stopping and starting even when playing along with a backing track or another instrument.

Understanding and internally feeling pulse/beat and knowing the difference between beat and rhythm are crucial for young musicians but not actively addressed in many methods.

3. Students Lack Imagination, Creativity and Curiosity

With everything laid out, page after page, students won't become very creative or curious about music. Children are naturally inquisitive, exploratory and creative. Let's encourage that in lessons. Few method books share quality activities to enhance these aspects of the learning process, which are critical skills we want our students to nurture and use throughout their life in all areas.

4. Students Are Nervous about Improvising

There will of course always be students young and old who are nervous about making up their own music, but you can significantly reduce the number of nervous students in your studio by making improvising a regular part of lessons right from the beginning. Just like singing, we want this to be a normal part of the lesson experience.

5. Students Don't Know or Understand Patterns

Patterns are to music like words are to text. When reading music effectively, good sight readers won't be reading every note (just as we don't read every letter while reading a book — we read by words). While method-book students may be able to read notes well, many stumble when asked to sight read or to quickly learn new material if common patterns aren't presented to them and actively explored in class.

Patterns can be melodic (Alberti bass, boogie pattern, scale passages, sequences) or rhythmic (tango, offbeat patterns, syncopations, Latin or rock grooves). And the more students are exposed to these and the more they explore and create with them, the better they'll read music.

Beginner Boredom Can Be Terminal

Working through page after page of method books can be really mind-numbing for students (*and* teachers!). Sure, some students love checking off new pieces, but it's been my experience that students — particularly beginners — crave other activities while working through a method book.

While the benefit of method books is that everything is laid out in front of you, using them for teaching is like riding a horse with blinkers/blinders on or like ten-pin bowling with the bumpers up — you'll only head in a very limited direction and likely not be taking much consideration of students' preferences.

If students are getting bored with their beginner lessons, they're not going to persist with lessons long enough to become what we hope they will become: musicians for life.

SELF-ASSESSMENT 1: Teaching Beginners

How imaginative, musical, creative and varied is your beginner teaching right now? To get an idea of where you're at, give yourself a rating from one to five for the statements in the following self-assessment, where one means 'not accurate about me at all' and five means 'accurately describes me'. Once you've rated yourself for each statement, total up your scores, then use the answer key to determine your next steps. When you complete this check-in, think about your *beginner lessons only*, up to the first six to eight lessons with a new student up to age 12.

Beginner Check-In Statements	Self-Rating (1–5)
I absolutely love teaching my current beginner lessons.	
I feel like my beginner lessons set students up for success in their future learning.	
I believe that the most important experience for young beginners at the piano is to be imaginative, creative, curious and exploratory.	

NO BOOK BEGINNERS

I develop students' playing by ear each lesson.	
In the first lesson, I encourage students to play me things they've taught themselves.	
The focus of my beginner lessons is fun, improvisation, creativity and exploration.	
I use stories as a basis for fun improvisations.	
When it comes to introducing reading, I use a variety of method books to suit students, but I don't introduce these until after a few weeks.	
Parents often tell me how happy they are with their child's beginner lessons and how much they are playing at home.	
I use a lot of analogies to teach technique at the beginner levels — rocket blast-off, lion paw, grasshopper jump, hot stove, sailing, painting, etc.	
My students and I happily sing in each lesson.	
My student feels and knows the difference between 3/4 and 4/4 metre.	
My student is happy to make something up at the piano with little instruction.	
Total	

What Your Score Means

Score: 0–25
It's Time to Update Your Method Book!

The bad news is you're likely teaching the way you were taught with a limited focus on reading, counting and slowly expanding note values and musical range. You may be using an older-style method that starts with both thumbs on middle C and has very little exploration or imagination built in. You may also be using the same method for every student.

The good news is that you're thoughtfully examining your own teaching style, which indicates an approach to lifelong learning. Now it's time to expand! I want to show you, in a step-by-step way, how you can integrate creative new musical experiences for students into the first lessons and have a more musical, exciting time. I also want to challenge you to explore modern approaches and use multiple method books that suit each student's goals.

Read this book with an open mind. Consider how implementing the NBB lesson ideas could radically improve outcomes for your beginners without upending everything you know (and love) about beginner teaching. You've got a solid traditional foundation upon which to build. Now let's break out of those shackles!

Score: 26-39
Using a Sequenced Approach Will Have Big Effects

If your score landed here, it means that you're already implementing some off-page or 'no book' ideas in your beginner lessons, but you can go much further.

You may still be relying heavily on a method book while supplementing with activities you've learnt from other teachers, conferences, workshops or online. Perhaps you throw in an occasional improvisation activity, break out an iPad app or use one of the many amazing games for teaching notes and rhythms.

What you're missing is a step-by-step approach that integrates all these activities into a sequenced learning plan that builds week to week and sets students up for a much deeper understanding of music when the time comes for reading.

Score: 40+
Watch Out for Shiny Objects!

You've got a lot of creativity in your lessons already and you're seeing great results from the beginners you teach. You may have created your own beginner approach that aligns or integrates with your favourite method. Kids are having fun and parents are happy.

You're the kind of teacher who loves your own learning — reading, watching videos, attending online webinars or in-person conferences and attending masterclasses. You're always trying new ideas to get the most out of your time with students, and you may even have thought about whether you should be sharing your ideas with other teachers!

But the downside of this enthusiasm is that you may also be finding that you are so excited about new ideas that you try too many new things and end up confounding your students. You fall into 'shiny object syndrome' where you're ready to jump on whatever the latest trend or idea is without fully integrating the last one. Reviewing old material sounds a little boring when there's so much new stuff to explore! (I know I've fallen into this trap before.)

This book will help you slow down your mind and bring structure to your approach. By following the sequenced lesson plans presented here and seeing how each builds on the last while expanding to new concepts along the way, you may be able to bring more order to your own approach.

Reconsidering the Reading-First Approach to Learning Piano

Let's think about what babies do when they're starting to learn how to speak. The first thing they do is they start making sounds. They start babbling: 'dada … baba … dah!' Musically, we'd call this *improvising*. Eventually, those sounds form into words, then sentences (melodies). They do a lot of listening at this time as well as a lot of copying and imitating.

So we have an established process for language acquisition: first listening, then making sounds, and then, eventually, reading and writing the language. But those two things are very much last on our list. Teaching music like a language is the foundation of the MLT approach from Dr Edwin Gordon that I talked about in the introduction. After a lot of research and trialling, I have no doubt at all that this is, by far, the best way to approach music learning for beginner musicians as well.

Before I take you through the nitty-gritty of the approach, however, I need to share the three core philosophies and mindsets that underpin *No Book Beginners*, which we'll explore in Part 2.

TAKEAWAYS

- ♪ In the 1850s, all musicians were creators *and* performers. Printed sheet music was not readily available, so musicians had to be able to improvise and compose.

- ♪ The advent of readily available sheet music in the early 1900s saw the training of musicians shift towards what we call the 'Performer Model'. Pianists were trained to perform the classics rather than being taught and encouraged to create their own music.

- ♪ Method books arose as an easy and convenient way to teach students to read music from their very first beginner lesson.

- ♪ The reliance on method books by music teachers has led to a persistence in technical deficiencies as students become more proficient at playing the piano.

- ♪ A focus on teaching beginners how to *read* rather than teaching them to *engage with music* means many potentially lifelong musicians are never making it beyond the beginner stage.

- ♪ I believe that beginners should learn music in the same way they learn a new language, and this is the basis of my *No Book Beginners* approach.

PART 2
Three Foundational Mindsets for Change

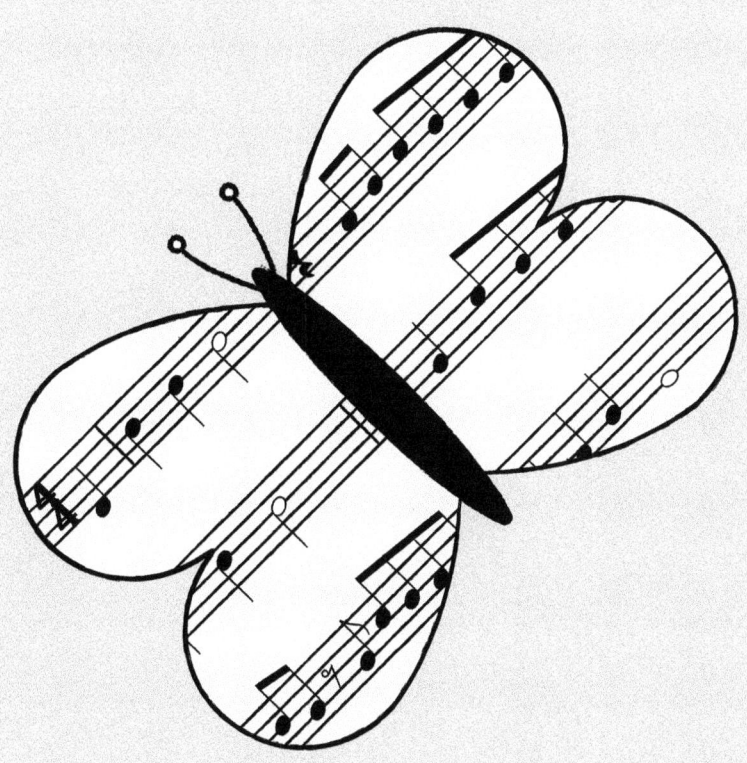

Before I start this part, it's important to note that I'm not advocating for students to stop learning to read music or for teachers to take on lots of non-readers in their studios. Teaching students who don't want to read music is a significant challenge; it's much harder to fill lesson content, and it can seem like you're not making much progress as there are no obvious benchmarks or milestones except perhaps a recital or performance.

But a flexible mindset can pay huge dividends.

Take the case of a teenage student I had once. I took Luke on as a transfer student. He enjoyed playing music he'd learnt through YouTube tutorials and was adamant he didn't want to learn to read music. Most teachers would simply request that Luke stop watching YouTube tutorials and start getting serious with music (learn to read) or find another teacher. But I wanted to see how this played out because I knew he was musical and enjoyed coming to piano lessons. I had a feeling I might just be able to change his mind.

Each time he'd start a new piece on YouTube, I'd find the sheet music. Each lesson would involve showing him what the music looked like, helping him find the best fingering, adding more dynamics and balance to his playing and pointing out things he was playing on the score. When he asked me if I could play something, I'd find the music and sight read it. He soon realised that by reading music he could learn things much faster than by watching tutorials.

Over time, I kept reminding him that reading the sheet music would make things so much easier. Eventually, he said, "OK, how long will it take me to learn to read music?"

I told him it would take the best part of a year but that he was already ahead of most students in that he knew his way around the piano and could already play confidently. Now it was about connecting the playing with how it looked on the page.

I also told him that it was going to be slow and frustrating and that he would be playing 'Twinkle, Twinkle, Little Star' and 'Hot Cross Buns' to get started but to not be dismayed; I'd move as quickly as I could to the more fun stuff. I needed his complete commitment if it was going to work because (and this is the important point) *there's no point forcing a teen or adult to read music if they don't want to.*

Excitedly, he agreed, and we got started. Sure enough, over the course of six months and with lots of focus, Luke slowly started to read the music he was trying to play. We continued to work on the YouTube music alongside the reading to keep his motivation high and I kept connecting the two as much as possible.

I share this story to highlight the importance of flexibility in teaching. If I'd told Luke that he needed to find a new teacher, I doubt he would have done that. And even if he had, I doubt anyone would have wanted to take on a teen who didn't read music. He may well have stopped playing in frustration and never turned to music again.

The sad fact is that many students who otherwise enjoy music and would love to play it into adulthood are discouraged and quit learning when teachers have a singular focus in lessons: reading. How do you shift your mind away from this singular focus? There are three core philosophies I subscribe to that I feel are important here.

1. A More Holistic Approach to Music Teaching

The way I like people to start considering a more holistic approach to music teaching is to think of an iceberg.

Above the waterline are the 'tip of the iceberg' skills of reading, performing and interpretation — and by implication, technique and theory — that have developed out of the Performer Model of the 19th and early 20th centuries. This is the content that method books are perfectly suited to help teachers deliver.

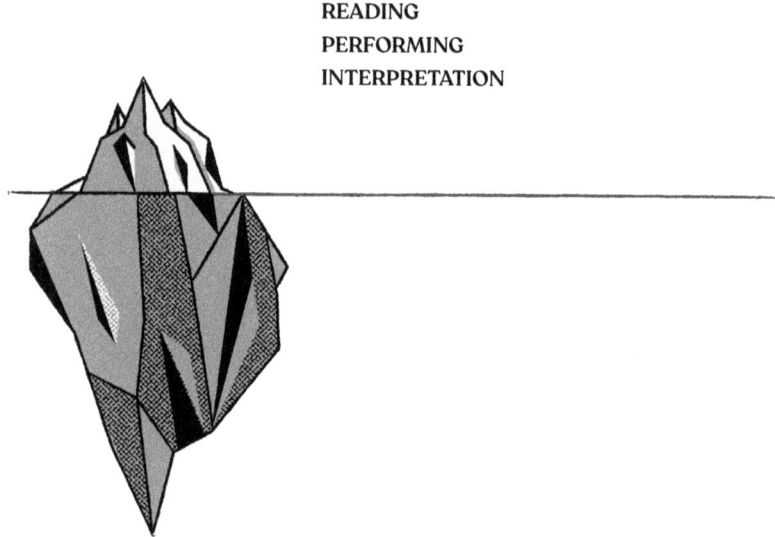

But what about the rest of the iceberg that we can't see?

Before we go on, I want you to think about what some

THREE FOUNDATIONAL MINDSETS FOR CHANGE

of the 'below the waterline' skills might be. What are the musical skills and activities you feel make up a holistic experience for piano students? You might also know them as 'functional skills'. Take a minute to grab a pencil and write below the waterline on the image on page 50, the skills you believe students should learn in order to be well-rounded musicians. Only look below when you've done it.

Done it? OK great!

I believe the bulk of what makes for a holistic music-learning experience are all the things below the waterline in the image below. These are what I consider to be the functional skills that many 'classical music lessons' ignore.

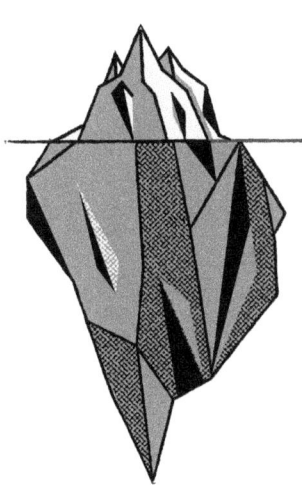

READING
PERFORMING
INTERPRETATION

COMPOSING
IMPROVISING
ARRANGING
PLAYING BY EAR
ACCOMPANYING
NOTATING

SINGING & PLAYING
READING LEAD SHEETS
JAMMING
PLAYING IN BANDS & ORCHESTRAS
EXPLORING OTHER INSTRUMENTS

Do some of the items below the waterline on the page 51 image match up with what you wrote below your waterline? Do you have others to add to the list?

These are the key creative music-teaching experiences and activities that I believe contribute to fostering all-rounder piano students. These are the skills that will allow our students to play in their school jazz band, compose music for a concert, accompany their friend singing, be confident in joining some friends in forming a local garage band, be more effective sight readers and be able to rearrange music and write it down.

Importantly, these are the very skills that the NBB framework introduces early in those critical beginner lessons so that things like singing, improvising and playing by ear become a normalised part of the lesson experience. If you feel like a lot of your teaching is 'tip of the iceberg' stuff, this book is here to help.

2. Student-Centred Teaching

Something I have a problem with in pretty much all aspects of teaching (music or otherwise) is that the classical tradition of pedagogy centres on the teacher being the 'wise sage'/'font of all knowledge' and children the empty buckets that need filling. This industrial view of school is now well and truly debunked in favour of an approach that puts the student at the centre of their own learning.

Looking back on my teaching, I realised that my creative-teaching approach developed from an openness to helping students learn what *they* wanted to learn. When I was a beginner teacher, if a student brought a pop song to a music lesson or asked to learn a piece of video game music, I'd go out of my way to help them. Why? Because I knew that those were the things that were going to keep this student learning and playing music.

Why have so many teachers in the past just waved away students who brought their own music to lessons? Well, firstly, because that's how they were taught. Anything less than the masterworks was not worth learning, especially if there wasn't any quality published sheet music. Secondly, a lot of teachers simply didn't know how to respond to music brought to lessons by students.

It was this flexibility in my teaching that enabled me to triple the size of the piano department at Whitefriars College, where I was teaching at the time. I suddenly became the 'cool' teacher who could help pupils learn fun pieces they wanted to learn.

Of course, this approach must be balanced with the skills that we know students need to learn (technique, note reading, playing a variety of genres, etc.), but it all comes down to one thing: being *student centred* in your teaching. Student-centred teaching is about being flexible and helping students learn things they want to learn as well as the things that you know they should learn. When you become a student-centered teacher, you'll naturally become more creative because you'll have to be flexible enough to respond to what students want to learn and to work out the best way of teaching something that may be too hard for a student.

THREE FOUNDATIONAL MINDSETS FOR CHANGE

 SELF-ASSESSMENT 2: How Student Centred Is Your Teaching Right Now?

In the following self-assessment, rate yourself on a scale from one to five on how accurate the statements are. One means 'not accurate at all' and five means 'most accurate'. Once you've rated yourself for each statement, total up your scores and then use the answer key following the self-assessment to determine your next steps.

Success Check-In Statement	Self-Rating (1–5)
I ask my students what their goal of learning piano is and check in at least annually.	
We work together to set short- and long-term goals at regular intervals.	
I believe in a varied approach to assess student progress that may include recitals, exams, performances, recordings and portfolios.	
I help my students learn music they want to learn.	
I encourage students to play me things they've taught themselves.	

NO BOOK BEGINNERS

I encourage students to learn things themselves from YouTube.	
My students only play in recitals when they make the decision to do so.	
If the music that students want to learn is too hard for them, I try to find ways to simplify it and help them learn what they can.	
I help students simplify music during the lessons instead of taking their music away and arranging it myself.	
I believe that teenagers and adults should be able to choose much of the repertoire they work on.	
I'm happy to help students improve pieces they are teaching themselves online.	
I ask students what they are learning in their free time and actively help them with these pieces.	
I make it a priority that the majority of the music my students learn is music they want to play.	
I demonstrate or share playlists of a variety of pieces so that students can choose pieces at the right level that they enjoy.	

I'm good at balancing time spent on the student's goals with time spent on my goals for them.	
Total	

What Your Score Really Means

Score: 0–35
Is Your Teaching about You or Your Students?

If you landed here, a small change in your approach will make a huge difference to your students' outcomes. Put simply, for most students, their motivation will be drastically enhanced by having choice in their learning.

You may have experienced your own lessons of simply being told what to play and how to play it. Each lesson was an experience in fault correction and reapplication to the given music. You likely heard other students playing the same music as you and saw them holding the same books.

This approach well and truly faded with the research behind self-determination theory making clear that autonomy is critical for motivation. Sure, there will be the one-percenter students who love to play classical music, practise six hours a week, perform in all your recitals and love every minute. But for the 99% of other students, flexibility and choice are crucial.

One of the simplest ways to improve your score here is to implement statements one and two in the self-assessment, about goal setting with any student over the age of 12. Students under this age will not be as critical about choice, but teens and adults need their own goals (which might not be the same goals as yours) to be front and centre.

Alternatively, choose one of the self-assessment ideas to implement with one student this week, and assess the results. Every step you take toward a more student-centred approach will have a big impact in the future.

Score: 36–49
Find the Balance

The great news is that you're already doing lots of things to give your students autonomy in their learning. You're giving them choices and letting them drive some of their lesson experiences.

What you need to strive for is the balance between the student's goals and what you know they need. This balance will be different for all students. It will also change over time.

Some students, especially adults, will need to have almost total say in what they do at the start. Others may not know what they want and will need you to help start them off. If your goals are not aligned, split your lesson time between working on their music and covering the skills you know they need to improve. This can be a fine balancing act, but it will pay off in spades with student rapport, practice and retention.

Also consider whether performing written music at recitals is the best goal for all your students. Perhaps some of your students are naturally more creative and would like to perform their own composition. Or perhaps they really don't like performing but could have a recording of their piece published on YouTube and shared on your website. Think about creative ways to get your students to participate without making them perform if they don't want to. Non-performers could contribute to recitals in other ways, such as handing out programs, doing the sound or lighting or running the PowerPoint presentation.

Score: 50+
Don't Lose Sight of the Big Picture

You may be finding that you're almost too student centred. (Yes, it's definitely possible!) Depending on the student, it's easy to focus too much on their goals and not on the skills they need to develop — touch, rhythm, reading, performance, interpretation, etc. — to the detriment of their learning. And when students don't feel they're making progress in their learning, they'll get disheartened and quit.

Now, this is a fine line to walk because you don't want to discourage students by forcing everything upon them, but you don't want them to take the lead totally. You're still the guide.

If you scored in this range, make sure that you've got firmly in mind the bigger-picture curriculum for your student. (For more on this, explore our free 'Ultimate TopMusic Guide to Intermediate Curriculum Planning for Piano Teachers' at topmusic.co/curriculum.) It's OK to focus more on their music for a few weeks, but perhaps then move to a more balanced approach. Like everything in music, balance is critical.

3. A More Creative Approach

As noted earlier, I believe that much of what is taught in a traditional music lesson is just the 'tip of the iceberg' of what an in-depth musical experience should be all about. So when we discuss teaching more creatively, what I'm talking about is actively exploring all the 'below the waterline' activities during lessons with students and making it an integrated part of the lesson experience.

Creative piano pedagogy involves any of the following activities. (This list is not exhaustive.)

THREE FOUNDATIONAL MINDSETS FOR CHANGE

- ♪ learning to sing and play at the same time
- ♪ experimenting with dynamics, articulation and swing
- ♪ improvising
- ♪ learning and playing chord progressions
- ♪ learning pop songs, especially through simplification by chords
- ♪ learning how to read lead sheets
- ♪ reharmonising lead sheets
- ♪ arranging music by changing left-hand patterns or exploring styles
- ♪ creating and notating compositions
- ♪ learning jazz basics.

I break the complexity of creative activities into three levels, which we'll cover in a moment. If you're new to creative pedagogy, I don't expect you to jump into helping your student build a composition from scratch — there are lots of simpler ideas to try first. It's about moving away from a strict classical lesson structure, with its focus on reading and high-level performing, to all the other great stuff that a musical experience consists of. We're going to explore these ideas in the context of a beginner lesson in Part 3, but keep in mind that these creative activities can and should be something you consider exploring in all students' lessons.

It's also important to note that many students who are only exposed to the 'tip of the iceberg' activities during their lessons will often gravitate 'below the waterline' in their own time by trying to play things by ear, teaching themselves music through YouTube videos or making up music themselves. This is all too true when I speak to adult students who learnt music as a child in a traditional setting. They'll talk about all the times that they, instead of practising what they were assigned, did things they knew their teacher disapproved of — making up bands with friends, playing songs from the radio, exploring all the sounds and beats in their keyboard, or just generally noodling around on their instrument. Maybe that describes you too?

My belief is that, far from being a waste of time, these creative experiences not only help to deepen students' understanding of music but also make them more likely to keep playing and learning music through adolescence and into adulthood. This is why creative activities are the basis of the NBB approach. By encouraging creativity from students in the first lessons, we show them that we're open to this manner of learning and happy to help them in their own creative endeavours.

I believe that creativity at an instrument is about more than just changing articulations, tempos or dynamics. To me, these changes are all about interpretation. You could, for example, use a lot of pedal when playing Bach, change the articulations of the melody of a Mozart sonata, swing a ragtime piece, or play something slower or faster. Sure, this is kind of creative, but I believe these are all still part of the 'tip of the iceberg'.

To help teachers understand my thinking about whether an approach is particularly creative, I've come up with what I call 'Three Levels of Creativity'.

In Level 1 (introductory creativity) students might explore simple changes to mostly non-melodic elements of a score:

- ♪ dynamics
- ♪ the octave (register) something is played in
- ♪ the feel
- ♪ the modality, from major to minor or vice versa.

These are simple but nonetheless creative activities any teacher can try with a student. Level 1 activities also don't require a huge amount of musical knowledge to be effective, which means that students of all levels and ages can try them. I believe Level 1 activities should be a regular part of good teaching for all teachers and students.

Level 2 activities are much more creative and require thinking and imagination along with a more concentrated knowledge of music. I call them 'contextual' as they are generally based on the music students are learning:

- ♪ taking elements of the repertoire and expanding them, exploring them, pulling them apart and putting them back together again
- ♪ changing the styles
- ♪ creating new introductions or endings for pieces
- ♪ adding improvisation in sections
- ♪ introducing new styles or feels to the pieces (such as changing the left hand from an Alberti bass to a tango accompaniment)
- ♪ reharmonising or arranging.

In Level 3, we move from using repertoire or provided works as a basis for creativity to creating music from scratch — i.e. composing. My TopMusicPro online professional development community provides frameworks for teaching Level 3 composition to students through my *12 Bar Blues* and *4 Chord Composing* courses, both of which require no prior or specialised knowledge. Students instead learn about harmony by doing, exploring and composing. Compositions don't have to be complex or complicated, especially when students are just starting. They also don't need to be fully notated, although there's nothing wrong with that as an activity if you have the time!

NBB lesson content incorporates all three levels of creativity, right from the first lessons, with a focus on Level 3. It may seem counterintuitive that the NBB framework is based mainly on Level 3 creativity, but that's because Levels 1 and 2 are based on repertoire that students haven't yet started.

SELF-ASSESSMENT 3: How Creative Are Your Current Piano Lessons?

In the following self-assessment, rate yourself on a scale from one to five on how accurate the statements are. One means 'not accurate at all' and five means 'most accurate'. Consider the questions as they relate to your early intermediate students who've been learning with you for a few years (not your beginners). Once you've rated yourself for each statement, total up your scores and then use the answer key to determine your next steps.

Success Check-In Statement	Self-Rating (1–5)
I sometimes start lessons with an interesting, creative activity: a game, quick improv, rhythm cup activity, pop song or clapback.	
My students love sharing things they've composed with me and will excitedly demonstrate them in the lesson.	
I'm happy to be flexible and adaptable in lessons and can sense when I need to change my lesson plan.	
I don't mind helping my students learn songs they are teaching themselves.	

THREE FOUNDATIONAL MINDSETS FOR CHANGE

I use creative activities — games, improv, chords, lead sheets — as fun ways to break up the lesson and provide enjoyable experiences.	
If I gave my students a scale that predominantly uses white notes to play in, they could create a four-chord progression and play it with style and rhythm.	
I encourage students to share pop songs they like with me so we can learn parts of them together.	
I teach my students cool pop riffs and well-known classical themes they can play to show off to their family and friends.	
My students can improvise a simple melody over a given chord progression.	
I love exploring black-key improvisations with my students.	
My students know the pentatonic and blues scales and can use them for a simple improvisation.	
I actively teach my students about chords, chord progressions and primary triads.	
I help students pull apart the harmony of their repertoire pieces by identifying chords and sometimes even writing the chords above the music.	

My students understand the basics of reading a lead sheet.	
My students could change the style of a piece they've learnt by changing the left-hand pattern (e.g. Alberti bass to boogie bass).	
I use backing tracks and drum beats more than the metronome to improve pieces, scales and technical work for intermediate students.	
Total	

What Your Score Really Means

Score: 0–30
Just Try One Thing

If you landed here, you should be congratulated on focusing on developing fine musicians who can perform with aplomb and who are learning to read with confidence. You're likely a classically trained teacher who focuses mainly on the 'tip of the iceberg' elements of music. You're a little nervous about 'making things up' or getting creative because it's not how you were taught. You likely work on similar music among your students and sometimes feel like you're in a hamster wheel of teaching.

The good news is that there is so much more to explore with your students and bringing in a little creativity will have a big impact on student motivation and (let's be honest) your own passion for teaching. While the *No Book Beginners* framework is a great way to get started, there's no shortage of creative ideas for students of all levels and abilities waiting at your fingertips.

I challenge you to try just one creative idea with one student in the coming week as a way to dip your toe in the water of this new way of teaching. The rest of the book will give you many ideas about the types of activities that work. Plenty more can be found at topmusic.co/blog.

Score: 31–44
Try a 'Repertoire Remix'

The great news is that you're already enjoying creative activities with your students and likely seeing the benefits.

One activity that you might not have explored is what I call 'repertoire remixing'. This is when you find a piece of music the student has already learnt that has a repeating left hand. Simple jazz pieces with walking bass lines often work well, but you can also find suitable pieces in classical and contemporary literature.

Once you've chosen a piece, play the bass line while the student improvises a new melody with their right hand. If the piece is jazzy, use a blues scale. If it's contemporary, use a pentatonic scale. If it's classical, use the piece's major or minor scale. Once the student is comfortable, they may play the left hand as well. Add a drum beat or play along on a second instrument. This is a great way to not only have fun but learn more about the way that melody is constructed and how key, melody and scales relate.

Score: 45+
Consider How You Can <u>Integrate</u> Your Creativity

You clearly have strong beliefs about the power of creativity in music teaching and are already using plenty of creative activities to deepen knowledge and inspire your students. Now it's time to consider how you can use creative activities to build connection and meaning in students to deepen their understanding of musical concepts.

The next time you're planning a new repertoire piece, see if you can find connections between the musical elements in the new piece and the following:

- ♪ similar elements in other sections of the same piece
- ♪ pieces the student has learnt in the past or other pieces currently under study
- ♪ activities the student enjoys outside of music — sport, dance, games, drama.

Then build your creative activities around unearthing and

strengthening those connections. Aim to create unique experiences that will form memories for the student and allow them to build on those connections in the future.[15]

What If I'm Not Creative?

This is a comment I hear *a lot*. Because so many of us have only experienced traditional 'tip of the iceberg' teaching as children, many teachers today don't think they have any creativity inside them. How sad is that? It's another reason why teaching the NBB framework is so important for students! We don't want our students to ever feel they're not creative. If you feel like this yourself, please believe me when I tell you that you *are* creative. You *do* have imagination. You just need a little nudge to bring it out of you.

In 2021, I invited Georgina, one of my TopMusicPro members and a teacher quite new to creativity in beginner lessons, on my podcast to chat about her experience using NBB for the first time in her studio. We were talking about the 'Around the World Improv' activity that is a feature of several weeks of the NBB framework.

In this fun activity, students are given a new five-note motif each week reminiscent of a culture around the world and encouraged to compose a simple melody based on the motif. As they move to new locations, they add their compositions to a 'passport' they create to share with their families at the end of the process. Remember the art class projects I mentioned in Part 1?

Georgina told me how her students had enjoyed this activity so much that she'd decided to take it a step further by adding stories to each of the motifs and locations. As you can tell, any doubts about her own creative potential had vanished:

> *I thought you could even expand that and get students to draw and perhaps colour pictures! It could build into even a half-day activity for a summer camp or a group program. The possibilities for this framework are only limited by your own imagination!*

One of the benefits of our TopMusicPro membership is how freely members share their ideas and resources. In one such case, Jacinta, one of our members, shared her own version of the 'Around the World Improv' passports she uses with her students and Georgina got inspired to try these out herself:

> *I decided to try an 'Around the World Improv' project for all my young beginners this half term in preparation for summer groups. I'm really new to improv, so it's a bit of a late start for me, but I've been practising them myself and having far*

THREE FOUNDATIONAL MINDSETS FOR CHANGE

too much fun before trialling it with my pupils. Today, it was day one, and it's going down a storm. We had so much fun. Somehow, I managed to improvise semi-confidently, and we now have world passports. And huge thanks to Jacinta for sharing the passport she created for the 'Around the World Improv.'

Georgina even created her own new resources for the 'Egypt' week of the improv challenge. (See Lesson 6 of the framework, outlined on page 128.) And this was from a teacher who originally doubted her creative chops:

I got a heap of A5 mini card scrapbooks for as much Egypt-related creativity as they can imagine. We listened to original Arabian music as well as film themes such as 'Alibaba', 'Arabian Nights', etc. I resisted the temptation to include The Bangles' 'Walk Like an Egyptian'! Best of all, we have Egyptian pharaoh headdresses for them to colour and make at home and to wear while they play their improvisations.

Georgina is such a great example of teachers getting inspired by my resources and making them their own with added imagination and creativity.

Just like Jacinta, Georgina happily shared the template for the Egyptian pharaoh headdresses that her students were creating for the 'Around the World Improv' inside the TopMusicPro community for other teachers to use. How cool is that? Keep in mind that none of these were my ideas, but I just *love* them! All I did was spark the creativity in our teachers, and I believe I'll do the same for you when you start using NBB. Sometimes it just takes the little spark you get from one of these lesson ideas to take you on an amazing journey with your students.

Here's how one of our team members, Rebecca, was sparked to build upon our NBB 'Breakfast Improv':

> *I have used 'Breakfast Improv' in multi-level, multi-age group lessons. I also used a similar idea to create our own improvised group piece, 'Bega Valley Boogie'. I conducted them clapping their town name in relays: 'Candelo', 'Merimbula', 'Tilba-Tilba-Tilba', etc. Then we each played the rhythm of their town on blues scale notes over the C minor–B-flat–A-flat–G7 progression in the NBB framework.*

Is It OK to Spend Time on All This Creativity?

Another common concern I hear from teachers is that, before joining our TopMusicPro online community, they worried that their crazy creative-teaching ideas were

THREE FOUNDATIONAL MINDSETS FOR CHANGE

'wrong'. Because the performer paradigm and 'tip of the iceberg' is so cemented in music teaching, it's easy to wonder if you're doing something wrong when you break the mould. When these teachers come into our online community, one of the biggest reliefs for them is to find out that the creative way they've been teaching is OK. Even better, they realise there's a whole community of similarly creative teachers out there doing the same thing. It's like finding your tribe! Far from being wrong, adding creative elements to your teaching is a much more *balanced* way, and I guarantee that your teaching (and students!) will be all the richer for it.

Now, you may be a little cynical about whether this 'creativity' thing is real pedagogy or a distraction from the important parts of learning an instrument. Some teachers have challenged me saying that pop music teaching, composing and playing lead sheets is like the 'junk food' of music lessons (with the main meals, by assumption, being historical repertoire and technique). But the reality couldn't be further from the truth. Dr Martha Baker-Jordan summed it up perfectly in her 2003 book *Practical Piano Pedagogy*:

> *Of what value would it be to teach the definitions of dynamic markings without having students observe such markings in their current repertoire? Or to have students learn complicated rhythmic*

patterns but never play them? All elements of music instruction must be consistently integrated so that students perceive all segments of music study as an integrated whole whose parts are all interrelated … **Teaching a student to compose integrates and complements the skills needed to become a proficient reader in ways that many other parts of teaching cannot.**[16]
[Emphasis is mine.]

Simply put, creativity is like the magic glue that can bind musical experiences and concepts together for students and help them form stronger meaning and connections.

The Benefits of a Creative Approach to Music Teaching

Here are a few more reasons why creativity should be at the forefront of music lessons today:

♪ **Student retention.** Students — particularly tweens, teens, and adults — will not hang around lessons long if they're not learning things they want to learn. Students today are not the same young children who started lessons years ago. Times have changed, and our teaching needs to change too.

- ♪ **Self-belief.** Being creative in lessons leads to more naturally creative students who believe in themselves. As said earlier, one of the reasons too many teachers believe they are bereft of any creativity is because it was so effectively beaten out of them as students to prioritise the pursuits of reading, performance, and classical-music interpretation.

- ♪ **More confidence.** Students who are exposed to a large variety of experiences in lessons have more confidence that they can do things themselves:

    Teacher: 'Could you work out a lead sheet?'
    Student: 'Sure — I did that in my lessons.'
    'Could you compose something in the key of G?'
    'Easy!'
    'Could you improvise along to this 12-bar blues?'
    'No problem!'
    'Some other students need someone to play keys in their band.'
    'Sure, I'll give that a go.'
    'Could you play "Happy Birthday" so we can sing along?'
    'Too easy!'

Getting Parents on Board with the Creative Approach

Because many adults today received a traditional classical-music lesson experience, they may unwittingly harbour some concerns about the creative non-reading approach you're taking with their child. If parents have been brought up to believe that piano teaching only occurs with a method book, they might need a little coaching. Perhaps they experienced piano lessons themselves as a child and expect that you will teach in a similar way to the way in which they were taught. As Australian composer Elissa Milne says:

> *If parents find this strange, tell them that it's much more important that you explore rhythm, pulse, creativity and improvisation before they start reading. I've never had a parent anything but thrilled to see their child exploring lots of sounds on the piano, using all the keys and pedals and having a ball.*[17]

So, we just need to educate them! Remind them about how much their child will benefit from getting these foundations right, and I bet you'll have them on your side. If not, you might want to reconsider whether this is the right family for your studio. Ask them if they want their child to love music and play for life. When they say 'Yes, of course', you can let them know that this is the best way to start. You can also share with them the quote from Dr Baker-Jordan. (See pages 75-76.)

TAKEAWAYS

- ♪ NBB does not advocate for students to stop learning how to read music; there is a better way to engage beginners before teaching them to read.
- ♪ For teachers, a flexible mindset can pay huge dividends as it opens you up to teaching more holistically, more creatively and in a more student-centred way.
- ♪ All these strategies will lead to better outcomes for your students and, thus for you as a teacher.
- ♪ All music teachers are creative and can teach creatively — whether they think they can or not.
- ♪ If you are already teaching creatively, you are not doing anything 'wrong.' In fact, you are ahead of the pack!
- ♪ You might encounter resistance from parents who expect their children to be taught in the same way they were taught. Reassure them about the benefits of a creative approach, possibly using the thoughts from Dr Martha Baker-Jordan and Elissa Milne to help.

Remember to get this!

If you have not done so already, make sure you visit our companion website at nobookbeginners.com, where you can watch videos of me teaching the NBB approach, download complete lesson plans for Lessons 1 - 5 of the framework and access all associated resources including backing tracks, sheet music, practice plans and much more.

DOWNLOAD NOW!

nobookbeginners.com

PART 3

The NBB Framework and Lesson Plans

So far, a case has been presented for why we need to bring creativity back into music lessons and why teaching note reading in the first lesson isn't the best way to introduce students to music. But the challenge of setting up this situation is that if you're a more traditional and classically trained teacher, even if you agree with the previous two sections and are keen to try teaching with no books, where do you start?

This section is dedicated to the implementation of the NBB framework in your own lessons. The great news is that all the difficult work has been done for you. Just as a method book steps you through teaching reading, the NBB lesson plans will step you through everything you need to do to teach creative beginner lessons *without* reading. There are ten complete NBB lessons you can use with any beginner, and this section shares the first five lesson plans so you can try them out in your studio right away.

The goal is that after reading this section, you'll be able to confidently teach the first five NBB lessons to your next beginner, and you'll know where to go to get Lessons 6 to 10 if you're keen to continue. Please note that, for practical purposes, not all supplementary resources (for example, teacher accompaniments and sheet music scores) that form part of these first lessons have been included. To access all the materials, including play-along backing tracks to share with your students, and to watch videos of me teaching each of these lessons at the piano, head to nobookbeginners.com.

Common Questions I Get Asked about the Framework

What Age Will This Work For?

It's designed for ages six to ten, but it will work a year above and below depending on the student's maturity. For five-year-olds and under, there is a preschool version of NBB available in the TopMusicPro membership. For ideas about teaching teen and adult beginner lessons, see Part 4.

THE NBB FRAMEWORK AND LESSON PLANS

Will It Work for Other Instruments?

While primarily created for piano, the ideas in the framework can definitely be adapted to suit other instruments. Here's what music teacher Susan shared:

> *I am primarily a voice teacher and teach a little piano but recently took over piano at a primary school where I was already teaching voice. I have had a large influx of students and have used NBB with all of my newbies. I've had great feedback from parents so far saying children have really enjoyed their first few classes. I've also been able to use a couple of elements in my voice classes, which has been great.*

How Long Will It Take?

This really depends on your student. For some students, the full ten-week framework may take only six weeks to absorb. For others, it may take up to six months. This is why you need to be flexible with your approach. If it's taking longer and you want to introduce some reading, you can do this at any stage and use NBB alongside your reading approach.

What about Practice?

One of the most common questions about NBB from teachers accustomed to teaching from method books is

NO BOOK BEGINNERS

'If my student doesn't have a book, how are they going to practise?' This is a legitimate question and one with a hard-fought solution.

Firstly, you're encouraged to move away from using the word 'practise' and instead try the word 'play.' Every student enjoys *playing*. The word 'play' sounds easy, fun and enjoyable, whereas 'practise' is just the opposite — hard, boring, slow, tiring. A simple change of word use can have a big impact.

Clearly, we want our students to be engaging with music between lessons by playing/practising, but what can they play if all the lessons are about creating and improvising? Well, thankfully there is a lot and I've done all the planning work for you. For each lesson in the framework, if you download the full lesson plans from nobookbeginners.com, you'll see practice activities clearly explained for each lesson:

- ♪ continuing to improvise along with backing tracks
- ♪ practising songs and chants
- ♪ practising rhythmic tapping and clapping
- ♪ and much more

THE NBB FRAMEWORK AND LESSON PLANS

Do I Have to Do Everything?

Like all my resources and thinking in teaching, I never want to direct that you must do this my way or you must do X, Y or Z. I much prefer to say, 'Look, here's an approach that I've used, and it seems to be working really well. I'm getting great engagement. I'm getting deep learning. Why don't you give it a shot?'

Using the framework allows you to continue teaching exactly as you do, but you can, of course, try some of these new ideas in your studio alongside what you're doing. Or you could go, 'You know what? I'm going to try this out with my new student. I think she is going to really enjoy it, so I'm going to try it for two to four weeks before I start with the method book.' Then, try out some of the activities shared in this NBB approach. My experience is that it makes a huge difference to both the fun you have in those first lessons and the deep learning that the student will get from delaying reading to later on.

One TopMusicPro member, Bec, shared how she uses NBB in her studio:

> *When I have a new student, I use NBB Lesson One as my first lesson. I print a NBB one-page ten-week plan and see where we end up! Some students come with such a strong plan of what*

> they want to play, so I follow their rabbit trails as necessary in the coming weeks. Some students are a bit of a mystery to me, and I stick to NBB quite closely until I suss them out. Some students do sections of NBB alongside repertoire or a method.

Do I Have to Go in Order?

Yes, the lesson plans in NBB are sequential, and each one builds and reinforces the learning of the previous week. While you can pull elements and activities out of any of the lessons to add them to your own way of teaching, I recommend taking a beginner through from the beginning. Whether you follow all ten lessons is totally up to you though.

Will It Work for Groups?

Absolutely! With a little extra creative thought and coordination, you can definitely make this work for groups. Here's one of our members, Rachel:

> This year I've been using the NBB method for all of my new students, and a majority of these have been in group lessons. I have a sibling group of three who are working together in one class, and last week I assigned them the 'Animal Improvisation Story' challenge found in Lesson

1. Today, when they came for lessons, their mum told me that this was one of the best practice assignments she had ever seen. She said, 'They were literally fighting over who was going to get to practise! It was a great problem to have, and they had so much fun!'

Core Fundamentals

The NBB approach is built on some core fundamentals. Here are the top five that underpin much of this framework and that I believe should underpin the lessons we teach for all our students.

1. The Primary Goal of Beginner Lessons Is Exploration, Creativity and Fun

If kids are out exploring a new forest or caves, they aren't going to want to sit and write about it; they want to engage, touch, smell, run, climb. That's what we want them to do at the piano as well (well, maybe not the climbing!).

A student's first piano lessons should be filled with fun and exploration — not only to open their minds to possibilities but also to encourage curiosity. A great first-week activity is having a look inside an acoustic piano, if one is available, and seeing how it works. What happens when you push the pedal? What happens if you sing into the strings with the pedal held down? What do the hammers and dampers do? These are all part of encouraging curiosity.

*At home playing my Yamaha keyboard.
I have no idea why I had a tea towel on my head!*

If students are learning on a digital piano, I encourage them to explore what all the buttons do and to try different sounds and rhythm patches. Sometimes it's simple exploration like this that can really fire a student's passion. I remember I was completely addicted to synthesisers when I was a teen, even though they were expensive at the time. I saved up for my first Yamaha keyboard — which was so old it had a wooden frame! — and then an Ensoniq ESQ-1, and I wouldn't stop playing them. I read all the magazines and even joined the Ensoniq Users' Group. While I might not have been formally 'practising the piano' as my teacher would've liked, I was creating, composing, developing my ear and learning to multitrack record my music. My connection with music and my musical identity was building.

2. Storytelling Is a Great Way to Get Creative with Children

In the framework, storytelling is often used as a gateway to helping students improvise without worrying if what they are playing is 'right' or 'wrong'. Connecting creativity with story can reduce a student's inhibitions and make the whole process much more organic and fun, particularly for reticent or shy students.

Georgina, who we met earlier, shared about how her students took the stories and improvisations in the 'Around the World Improv' to another level in her studio, going as far as creating costumes to go along with them:

> We had masks, headdresses, alien costumes. It was just wonderful, and we made stories with each improvisation. We played around with it in the

lesson, and then they had to go home and try and make a musical story. They would come back the following week and play me the musical story, and I had to guess what was going on. We had thieves and robbers around pyramids, and they completely blew me away with how they interpreted it.

This is an example of how teachers can expand and develop the ideas presented in the NBB framework and make it into something completely innovative and imaginative. Every student and studio that explores NBB has different outcomes, which is why it's so exciting.

3. Technique Is Important, but Don't Worry If It's Not Perfect at First

I know, I know — controversial. I certainly admire teachers who have the patience to (and work with the type of student who can) work for weeks on getting a hand lift absolutely perfect or who can work for weeks on the perfect two-note slur. In an ideal world, with dedicated students and parents to support them and hours of practice time spent every week, I'd focus on this too. But what I've found is that most of today's students simply don't have the time or patience to be able to experience and practise this level of detail in their early lessons. And sadly, if they don't have the time or patience to focus on this but it's the primary goal of your teaching, there is going to be a mismatch and they'll be more likely to quit prematurely. The unfortunate result is that all the time you painstakingly spent making sure their technique was perfect will have been wasted anyway.

I prefer to advocate an approach of getting just the basic techniques right first. NBB teaches students how to sit properly at the correct height, using the correct wrist and finger movements. I like getting students to teach their parents[18] how to do this as a fun activity at home, then refine it over time as they build confidence and get more experience.

I see a lot of concern from teachers about 'buckled knuckles' (where the first joint of the finger bends backwards when students press down on keys) or 'flying pinky fingers' (where their little fingers are held permanently in the air). Of course, these are not ideal, but these issues tend to work themselves out over time as students grow and gain strength and as their bodies physically change.

4. Music-Making Should Be Social

What's the secret to building a lifelong connection to music? I know, it's a big question! One of the key factors that contributes to students forming a love for and a lifelong connection to music is playing with others. The social aspect of music-making is critical to enjoyment.

So, in NBB there are lots of duets and backing tracks, echo play, clapbacks and singing and chanting together.

Most of my strongest memories of playing music as a child, teenager and young adult are when I've played with other people. I wonder if it's the same for you? Think back to your early years as a musician. What do *you* remember the most?

Playing a duet with my sister, Sally, at the end of a recital in Miss Mac's house with my brother, Chris, looking on.

5. Singing and Movement Are Everyday Parts of Music Learning

I want my students to know that singing and moving to music is just a part of how we do things in music education. If you can get students singing and moving around the room and clapping and tapping and chanting and all those kinds of things right from those first lessons, it becomes normalised, so students don't have to feel awkward about it because 'It's just how we do things around here'.

The NBB Lesson Plans

Have you ever taken the time to consider your main teaching goals for a beginner piano student? What would you like to impart in these important first lessons? What musical concepts are vital to experience and explore? What mindset and beliefs do you want to engender? What can you leave out for now?

Before you go on, set aside five to ten minutes to think about this, and jot down your ideas in the table of 'General/Mindset Goals' and 'Musical Goals' over the page. Once done, compare your goals to the ones used in the NBB framework, and see where they are different or similar.

My Beginner Teaching Goals

General/Mindset Goals *What do I want my students to think/feel about music learning?*	**Musical Goals** *What musical skills do I want my beginner students to develop in the first five to ten weeks of lessons?*

THE NBB FRAMEWORK AND LESSON PLANS

Here are the 'General/Mindset Goals' that the NBB framework seeks to impart in the first ten weeks:

- ♪ I love music and I love teaching students.
- ♪ Music lessons are creative and exploratory.
- ♪ Creating music is both fun and easy.
- ♪ You can use music to tell stories.
- ♪ Making music with others is fun.
- ♪ The student is a musician.

How did your goals align? Even if they were way off, hopefully the NBB list has given you food for thought. And if they're in alignment, then you're in the right place!

So, what about the 'Musical Goals' you'd like your beginners to work towards? Here are the more specific musical skills that NBB seeks to develop. By the end of ten weeks, students should be able to do the following:

- ♪ Sit properly, at the correct height, and correctly use the arm, wrist and fingers.
- ♪ Improvise on black and white keys in time with an accompaniment and come to rest on a suitable tone.
- ♪ Tell a story with music.
- ♪ Feel a steady sense of pulse.

- ♪ Explain and demonstrate the difference between 3/4 and 4/4 time.
- ♪ Sing and play common rhythm patterns.
- ♪ Tap a rhythm and keep a beat at the same time.
- ♪ Sing a song and keep a beat on their knees at the same time.
- ♪ Name all the white notes and find them quickly.
- ♪ Discuss the basics of harmony and how bass lines can outline a 'home' key.
- ♪ Discuss how chords, patterns and melodies can be repeated to create music.
- ♪ Transpose music into different keys (without too much trouble if they know a few tricks).

Phew! That's a big list. The best thing is that all these objectives can be explored through experimentation, play and improvisation without any reading. Obviously, these musical skills will continue to develop over time past the beginner lessons, but we want to set the examples of these as early as possible.

So, how did yours align? Regardless, I hope you're excited to see how the NBB lesson plans can help achieve these goals in ten weeks.

***

THE NBB FRAMEWORK AND LESSON PLANS

With our goals aligned, let's explore the plans for Lessons 1 to 10. Here's what to expect:

- ♪ Lessons 1 to 3 have a full lesson plan and practice plan detailed.
- ♪ Lessons 4 and 5 have a full lesson plan.
- ♪ Lessons 6 to 10 have an overview so you can get a feel for how the topics introduced at the start develop over time.

As I mentioned earlier, many more teaching and student resources are available online to support your teaching in this innovative new way:

- ♪ teacher accompaniments for all the improvisations
- ♪ fully orchestrated backing tracks
- ♪ videos of me at the piano showing you exactly what to do for each of the ten lessons
- ♪ detailed practice plans for your students for each week
- ♪ the music for the rote-learning piece
- ♪ lists of extra resources, articles and products to enhance your teaching
- ♪ the complete lesson plans for Lessons 6 to 10

If you'd like to access the complete NBB online course with all these inclusions, come and join us inside TopMusicPro by going to topmusicpro.com.

Lesson 1

Objectives

- ♪ Get your student excited to explore the piano, and start building rapport with them.
- ♪ Help them understand how to sit properly at the piano.
- ♪ Explore improvising on the black keys. This is fun for the child and allows you to assess their musicality, listening skills and ability to follow instructions.
- ♪ Ensure that the child has things to go on with at home.

Things to Remember

- ♪ Be as excited and enthusiastic as you can possibly be!
- ♪ Encourage and praise lots.
- ♪ Have fun!

Lesson Plan

Getting to Know You

- ♪ Welcome the child to your studio. Show them around. Ask them about their favourite TV show, sports, things they do on the weekend, movies, food, colours. Have a chat!

- ♪ Get to know the child. You'll be able to refer to this and make connections in subsequent lessons.

- ♪ Depending on the child's age, I always like to ask them why they decided to learn piano. What do they love about music? What music do they listen to?

What can you play?

- ♪ Ask them if they'd like to play something. If they hesitate, tell them it doesn't matter how simple it is — anything is good.

- ♪ Be encouraging no matter how it sounds or how bad their hand position is!

- ♪ Show interest and excitement that they are already playing. This lets them show you what they can do and gives you a chance to assess their approach to the keyboard, their rhythm, technique, musicality and music they like.

Exploring 'What Can You Play?'

- ♪ If they can play something, I tend to work with them a little more on it. For example, if they can play 'Chopsticks', then I'll accompany them. If they can play 'Mary Had a Little Lamb', I'll play along with some chords. If they can play part of a song melody from the radio, I'll ask what it is and try to play along. Maybe we'll watch the video of the song on YouTube so I can make a connection with it and play something at the same time.

- ♪ Whatever they can play, see if you can enhance it with an accompaniment somehow.

- ♪ Don't worry too much about technique at the moment. This activity is about playing and making music.

How to Sit at the Piano

Now it's time to help the student sit correctly at the piano. Helping the student find a comfortable sitting position is vital in Lesson 1. Make sure that parents also know the right position so they can help their child get set up properly at home.

- ♪ Get the bench height correct first. Use a footrest if the child is small and show them how to place their shoulders, arms, wrists and fingers on the keys. (See the online lesson video.)

THE NBB FRAMEWORK AND LESSON PLANS

- ♪ Introduce them to 'Linda Ladybug' — a small rubber ladybug/ladybird toy that I use to help students understand a naturally curved hand shape at the piano while being a little bit of fun.[19] Linda is going to help you check your student's arm and hand position as she travels down the student's arm, from the shoulder to under their hand, and checks to make sure everything is in a comfortable, natural position.

- ♪ Put Linda on their shoulders and explain that she likes it when shoulders are relaxed. You can get them to hunch up their shoulders and then relax them. Give them cues for when you're not around. ('What would Linda think of this position?')
- ♪ Now, move down to the arm (parallel to floor), wrist (parallel to floor or slightly angled down), first set of knuckles/bridge of hand

(strong) and fingers and thumb (comfortably shaped).

- ♪ Finally, ask them to lift up the garage door (thumb), as Linda is going to crawl under their hand, which should give them a perfect hand shape. Remind them that they can also check this by placing their hand over their knee, then bringing it up to the keyboard in the same shape.
- ♪ Demonstrate *lots*. Students love to copy and will often do it perfectly.
- ♪ Demonstrate the wrong way and get them to correct you. Kids love this, especially the more over-the-top you act out the mistakes! Have fun with it.

Improvising on the Black Keys

Time to get creative!

- ♪ Let the student know that they are going to be playing on the black keys. Show them that the black keys are divided into groups of two and three notes. Can they play all the pairs of black notes up and down the piano (playing notes together with fingers 2–3)? What about the groups of three black notes (with fingers 2–3–4)?
- ♪ Have the student try playing the notes separately starting with all the black-key pairs,

making sure that they are always playing in a detached style. Avoid legato playing for this first period of beginning teaching. For background, method book author Dr Julie Knerr Hague discusses the importance of non-legato articulation for young beginners in one of her mini essays.[20]

♪ Demonstrate a non-legato touch with a light arm bounce.

♪ Find the improvisation accompaniments at nobookbeginners.com. Explain that you're going to play some cool accompaniments in a variety of styles, either on a second instrument or as a secondo part on the student's instrument (in a low register).

♪ Students need to listen to the 'feeling' of the accompaniment and then decide how their improvisation might go. Timid students might start on just one black note. Are they feeling the mood? Are they in time? Are they trying to do too much? Help them out.

♪ Make sure they are sitting correctly and using a non-legato touch.

♪ Try exploring loud and soft. Demonstrate by playing the accompaniment loud or soft. Try short and jumpy. What about slower/faster? Can they change their approach to suit? Are they listening?

Animal Improvisation Story

- ♪ A great way to get young children improvising in their first lessons is through the lens of animals.

- ♪ Have the student explore the different registers of the piano by demonstrating rumbling down low versus twinkling up high. Ask, 'What animals would you associate with these areas of the piano?'

- ♪ Teach the different sounds and registers of the piano. 'Which animal is the sound at the top of the piano? Which one lives down the bottom end? What's in the middle? What animal is slow and heavy? What animal is quick and jumpy?' Make fun sounds and lots of music. The student may like to use the pedal or not. Again, keep exploring.

- ♪ Guide the student through a story, demonstrating possible sounds, then having the student play and improvise. 'Let's choose two animals to make a story — for example, an elephant and an ant. What's going to happen? The elephant comes walking along.' Make big plodding sounds down low on the keyboard in steady rhythm. 'Then, he sees all the little ants running around.' Make twinkly sounds up high. 'Then, several ants run down the piano to him.' Play a glissando. 'He gets freaked out and tramples them.' Make a final-sounding squashing sound. 'The end!'

♪ Kids love creative activities like this, so make up your own with your student and have a ball.

Summary

♪ Thank the student for their story and all their beautiful playing.

♪ Finish the lesson on a high note, give encouragement and set tasks for the week.

♪ It's great to ask two questions at the end of any lesson: 'What did you most enjoy about your lesson today?' and 'What's one thing you've learnt about music today?'

Practice Plan

♪ The student teaches their parent how to sit at the piano and how to shape their hands. Students love being the teacher. This task reinforces posture and technique, and it will require continued refinement over the coming weeks and months.

♪ Have the student continue to explore black-key improvisations using backing tracks.

♪ Have the student choose two or three new animals for a new story at the piano. The student should make them contrasting (such as a bird, duck and bee).

Lesson 2

Objectives

- ♪ Build rapport and have fun.
- ♪ Revise technique and sitting position.
- ♪ Continue exploring improvisation, moving from black keys to white keys.
- ♪ Teach the student to recite words in time to a beat.
- ♪ Have the student learn to pitch-match on the piano.
- ♪ Have the student learn to keep a beat and move to music.
- ♪ Have the student learn where the C–D–E group is in any octave/register.

Things to Remember

- ♪ Always practise the lesson ideas before you teach.
- ♪ Check that you can play the accompaniments confidently.
- ♪ Practise the 'Singing/Echo Playing'. You'll need to be able to sing a simple melody while playing the blues comp.

THE NBB FRAMEWORK AND LESSON PLANS

Lesson Plan

Getting to Know You

- ♪ Find out what the student did over the weekend. What was their highlight? What did they enjoy most in their piano practice?

Review Sitting Position

- ♪ Before they play their animal improv, check posture. Swap spots, then sit poorly at the keyboard. Ask your student to teach you the correct posture and hand position.

- ♪ When finished, swap back, then have them show you a beautiful position, ready to demonstrate their animal improv. Get Linda Ladybug out, and remind the student she's watching. (I like to sit her on the piano watching sometimes!)

Improvising – Black Keys and Animal Improv

- ♪ As a warm-up, replay the black-key accompaniments from Lesson 1, and see how the student has improved. Give lots of praise.

- ♪ Try the new black-key accompaniment for Lesson 2 if you'd like variety. (See the 'Rhythm Ideas' section.)

- ♪ Before you ask the student to play their new animal improv, ask them what animals are in the story. Your job is to then work out the story by listening.

♬ Once they've played, tell them what you heard. Was it right? Was that their story? Could they try something different to tell the story more clearly?

Rhythm Ideas

♬ Play some music in 3/4 and 4/4 time and have the student clap and/or walk in time to the beat. Make it easy at first, then harder as they catch on. Assess how they feel rhythm. You can also play music from YouTube/Spotify/iTunes in a variety of styles. Can they tell the difference? If so, can they explain or demonstrate it?

♬ Can they keep clapping the pulse when you stop playing?

♬ It's great to give students an understanding of the difference between duple and triple metre (or march versus waltz), so play a steady march-like figure, and ask them to march on the spot along to it.

♬ Then, change to a waltz accompaniment while keeping the beat steady, and ask the student if marching to this beat still works. Hopefully, they'll realise it won't, so you can help them move between left and right foot on each of the downbeats. This is triple time (waltz).

- ♪ You could explain that one is counted in groups of two steady steps, while the other is counted in groups of three steps. Can they count the steady steps with you out loud?

- ♪ Try playing some other examples, either on the piano or using a recording, and have the student shift their weight to feel where there are stronger steps and weaker steps.

- ♪ If they're going well, they can clap or tap the other steps of the measure while moving their feet to the strong steps (downbeats).

Singing and Echo Playing

- ♪ Using 'Improv Accompaniment No. 1' from Lesson 1 (the G-flat blues), play the G-flat chord accompaniment with walking bass. Sing a simple one-note melody using only G-flat, while you play. Ask the student to copy you by singing back the melody. Stick to just the G-flat chord for now.

- ♪ When they can sing it, ask them to play it back while you play the accompaniment. Increase the melodic complexity as the student gets better. Add a note, start on a different note etc.

- ♪ You can also play the left-hand walking bass with the melody in your right hand for the student to either play or sing.

♪ Then, swap roles: play the accompaniment while your student plays or sings a melody for you to copy.

Frog and Snake (C–D–E) and White-Key Improv

♪ One of the best ways to get students to practise finding similar white keys up and down the piano is a game called 'Frog and Snake'.[21] The easiest way to understand this game is to watch the three-minute video on YouTube, but here's a quick overview. The student sits in front of the piano with the teacher on their right-hand side. The game starts when the teacher asks the student to play all the Cs from the bottom of the piano to the top, jumping in a nice, high arc (like a frog between lily pads) between keys. When the student plays the highest C on the piano, they have to jump back down via all the Cs again, but this time their teacher (the snake) is going to try and beat them to the bottom by quickly playing a scale of all white keys from the top of the piano down to the bottom. If the snake catches up with the frog, the teacher wins and the game can restart. Try this activity with your student and get them used to finding C first.

♪ Next, have your student try finding D. I call it the 'Dog in the Kennel' – between two black keys. Then, have them find E.

♪ When they can find C–D–E, ask them to play a simple improv on any set of C–D–E white keys while you accompany them using a white-key accompaniment. Keep playing in a detached style.

Song Rhythm

Teach your student the words to a simple folk song by rote and have them copy you. I like to use 'Rocky Mountain':

♪ Tap on your thighs (pat) while you say the words to keep a beat and have your student do the same.

♪ This week, have your student just learn the words in time with the beat (with no singing yet).

Practice Plan

♪ Keep exploring the black- and white-key improvs. Make sure students have backing tracks to continue using at home.

♪ Have the student practise being the frog finding different notes on the piano. Let the student know that you'll be testing them next lesson, and the snake is going to be extra fast!

♪ Have the student practise moving to other music during the week. Have them think about the following questions: 'Is it duple or triple?' and 'Can you count out loud?'

♪ Have the student practise saying the 'Rocky Mountain' words while keeping a steady beat on their legs. Have them think about the following questions: 'Is "Rocky Mountain" duple or triple metre?' and 'Can you step in time with the beat while saying the words?'

THE NBB FRAMEWORK AND LESSON PLANS

Lesson 3

Objectives

- ♪ Continue working on singing and pitch matching.
- ♪ Start teaching the rest of the white keys: F–G–A–B.
- ♪ Introduce the idea of transposing.
- ♪ Get students to play by ear.
- ♪ Add left-hand bass notes to a melody.
- ♪ Teach the student to audiate (inwardly hear) the words of a song while clapping a steady beat.[22]
- ♪ Teach the difference between *beat* and *rhythm*.

Things to Remember

- ♪ Don't rush. This plan is really flexible. You might only have completed half of Lesson 2 so far. Keep developing things slowly, at the student's pace.
- ♪ I haven't included the 'Getting to Know You' and 'Summary' sections. These are a given for all future lessons.

Lesson Plan

Frog and Snake (F–G–A–B) and White-Key Improv

- ♪ Test how well the student has learnt C–D–E using the 'Frog and Snake' game.
- ♪ Introduce them to F–G–A–B, and see how well the frog can bounce up and down the keyboard.
- ♪ Have the student try improvising using any white keys while you play any of the 'White-Key Improv' backings from Lesson 2.
- ♪ For another game to reinforce the newly learnt white keys, the student shuts their eyes, plays a note, opens their eyes and then sings and names the note.

Playing by Ear and Transposing

- ♪ Ask the student if they know 'Mary Had a Little Lamb'. Sing 'Mary Had a Little Lamb' together starting on B-flat. If this is an unfamiliar tune, do they know any other simple folk tunes ('Row, Row, Row Your Boat', 'Greensleeves', even the opening theme to Beethoven's Fifth Symphony)?
- ♪ Ask the student to play 'Mary Had a Little Lamb' on the black keys (starting on B-flat) by ear. Show them where to start. Help them as needed.

THE NBB FRAMEWORK AND LESSON PLANS

♪ If they can do it easily, try 'Twinkle, Twinkle, Little Star', 'Three Blind Mice', or 'Old MacDonald Had a Farm' starting on G-flat. Adjust the level of difficulty to suit the child.

♪ Explain to them that we can actually play the same tune starting anywhere on the piano. For example, play the note E, and sing 'Mary Had a Little Lamb' with them again, now in the key of C major. Then, have them try playing the song again by ear in the new key.

Singing and Echo Playing

This week will build on the echo singing and playing you did in the last lesson over the G-flat blues.

♪ Taking it a step further, you can now try call and response. Explain to the student that music is often like a conversation between two people. (I often do an over-the-top operatic example of question-and-answer singing!)

♪ Try a call and response. You continue to play the accompaniment and sing or play a little 'question'. The student, instead of copying you, responds back with an 'answer'. Have fun with it, making it harder/longer as the student progresses.

Rhythm Patterns and Clapping

- ♪ Test the student's ability to move to duple- and triple-metre pieces, either played on the piano or by recordings.

- ♪ Clap simple patterns in 2/4 and 4/4 using quarter and eighth notes (crotchets and quavers). You clap or tap and they copy, keeping a steady beat. You can also do this with vocal sounds: 'bah', 'bum' (funnier), or 'dar'. Kodály teachers might like to use 'ta' for quarter notes and 'ti-ti' for eighth notes.

- ♪ Have the student clap three beats and then a rest on the fourth beat. Then, have them clap two beats and rest two beats. Build up to clapping four beats and feeling four rests before clapping again.

- ♪ Set up a 4/4 pattern fun duet. Clap beats 1, 2, and 3 and have the student clap beat 4. Or clap beats 1 and 3 and have the student clap beats 2 and 4. It's heaps of fun.

- ♪ You can continue these ideas throughout the next lessons.

Beat and Rhythm

- ♪ Revisit the words to 'Rocky Mountain' while tapping a steady beat.

- ♪ Then, have the student clap the rhythm of the

words instead of saying them. Ask the student to put the words in their head (audiate).

♪ Explain the difference between *beat* and *rhythm*. Keep the beat while the student claps the rhythm, then swap.

♪ For a challenge, the students can clap the rhythm and keep a beat with their feet. Alternatively, they can tap the rhythm with one hand and keep the beat with the other. Then they can swap hands.

Practice Plan

♪ Have the student practise tapping the rhythm and keeping the beat of 'Rocky Mountain'.

♪ Have the student practise being the frog finding different notes. They should also practise eyes shut playing, singing and naming white keys.

♪ Pick one of the nursery rhymes used for the transposition exercise and have your student learn it starting on a few different notes that you specify.

♪ Have your student make up some new rhythms to clap while keeping a steady beat. They can prepare three to show you at the next lesson.

Lesson 4

Objectives

- ♪ Continue teaching the white keys through games.
- ♪ Have the student play by ear more.
- ♪ Continue to explore transposition.
- ♪ Guide the student to sing a simple folk song while keeping a steady beat.

Things to Remember

- ♪ Don't forget to keep checking posture and hand position.
- ♪ Lots of singing is important to make this a normalised part of the lesson experience as students get older.
- ♪ If students want to play something for you, let them do it and encourage it!

Lesson Plan

Transposing

- ♪ Listen to the transpositions you requested last week. Add a simple accompaniment of chords.

- ♪ If they haven't already done it, have the student try playing and transposing one of the harder songs (such as 'Old MacDonald'). Keep playing along with the student.

Improvising Concert!

- ♪ Ask the student to choose their favourite improvisation from the last three weeks. You might like to play through each of them again.

- ♪ Explain that you'd like to make a little concert out of that one piece, which they can perform for their family.

- ♪ When they've chosen their favourite, help them put together a simple arrangement of the piece. Add an intro and coda. Mix up the chords or accompaniments. (The provided accompaniments are only examples and ideas of what you can do.) Possibly combine improvs, such as playing them back to back in an A–B–A form. Decide on a few of their favourite improvisation 'licks' (riffs that they like when they improvise) and use them a few times.

- ♪ Run through the complete performance. If they'd like to play this at home, record the backing track they'll need to perform it.

- ♪ Students can also use this to play in school music class or at a school assembly.

White-Key Games

- ♪ Test how the student is going with finding, singing and playing white keys.

- ♪ Depending on their age, they can now try spelling words on the piano. Demonstrate by playing something simple like D–A–D. Ask the student what the keys spelled. Try another, then get the student to play-spell a word for you to say. Examples: F–A–D–E, B–E–E–F, F–E–E–D, B–E–A–D, D–E–A–D, B–A–G–G–A–G–E.

- ♪ Also have them try to sing the words too.

Singing

- ♪ Have the student recite the 'Rocky Mountain' words from memory while keeping a steady beat. Can they clap the rhythm? Reinforce the difference between *beat* and *rhythm*.

- ♪ When they can say the words, show them how the tune goes, then have them sing it with you. Play along with a simple rhythmic vamp using tonic and dominant chords in F.

- ♪ Show them how to find and match the pitch of the starting note on the piano and ask them to continue singing the song this week.

Lesson 5

Objectives

- ♪ Start teaching a new piece of music by rote: 'Thunder Showers'. Make this *big* news!
- ♪ Continue developing a non-legato touch.
- ♪ Confirm the student's seating position and posture.
- ♪ Get the student to hear and sing bass lines.
- ♪ Add a left-hand part to a simple tune.

Things to Remember

- ♪ This is a great time to recap all that you've been teaching. Play some 'Frog and Snake'. Ask your student to play random notes as quickly as possible. Do some call and response.
- ♪ Keep quizzing them on knowledge you want them to remember from previous lessons. That's the best way to make sure it sinks in.
- ♪ Keep checking posture and technique.

Lesson Plan

Quick Intro: White-Key Games

- ♪ Ask your student to show you what words they can spell on the white keys. Then, give them one back.

Harmony – Bass Lines

- ♪ Pick one of the transposition nursery rhymes you explored in the last lesson.
- ♪ Play along with the student with some simple fifths in the left hand.
- ♪ When you've played it once, ask the student to sing the note that sounds like 'home'. For example, if you've been playing 'Mary Had a Little Lamb' starting on B-flat, they should hear that G-flat is 'home' (the tonic). Have them play the note they've sung.
- ♪ Then, ask them to play that note with their left hand low on the piano. This is the start of exploring harmony. Can they play the melody and the left-hand bass note (one per measure)?
- ♪ Ask them if there is a place in the melody where it sounds like the bass note could change. Play the melody and help them sing the left-hand bass note and work out another note that would sound good to sing.
- ♪ They may say it's on the second 'little' of 'Mary had a little lamb, *little* lamb …' Hopefully, they find the D-flat (dominant) on their own. Can they sing the two notes while you play? If not, help them experiment. You could play the melody and they could alternate between other black keys.

- ♪ Keep exploring this idea with students: always singing, playing and discovering.

Play by Ear

- ♪ After they know 'Rocky Mountain', it's time to try playing it by ear.
- ♪ Have the student play the entire piece on the note F first, then help them work out where the notes change and where they move to. Depending on your student, they might do this easily or it might take several weeks.
- ♪ Ensure they don't play legato. A gently detached and relaxed touch is better for beginners. (See Lesson 1.)

First Rote Piece: 'Thunder Showers' (by Paula Dreyer)

It's time for your student to learn their first piece of music. Make a big thing of this! You're going to teach it by rote (demonstrating and the student copying). The student does not read the music; it's provided for your reference only. Over the page is the score (a full-page version can be found online at nobookbeginners.com):

NO BOOK BEGINNERS

'Thunder Showers' by Paula Dreyer from Little Gems for Piano: Primer Level. Copyright © 2016 pauladreyer.com. Used with Permission.

How to teach the piece:

1. Play the entire piece in the most beautiful way as a demonstration. The student should listen carefully while watching you (not the music).

Play the piece twice if they seem to enjoy it. They probably won't believe they'll be getting to play it!

2. Show them the positions in the right hand. Ask them to watch as you play the right hand again and have them tell you what's happening in the right hand. (There is alternation between two and three black keys.) Show them which fingers to use, and use a fluid motion with a forward roll at the end to move to the next block.

3. Help the student practise the right-hand movements. Then, show them how to use the pedal. If they're very little, either use a pedal extender or have them half stand up.

4. Make sure you and the student are keeping a steady beat. Count in, or they can try counting in.

5. Teach all the right hand this lesson and ask them to find the similarities and differences between the phrases. Teach by demonstrating and asking lots of questions.

6. Before the end of the lesson, perform the piece again for the student and then have them play through the right hand while you play the left hand.

Lesson 6

Lesson 6 continues with the rote piece, incorporates more harmony and introduces 'The Breakfast Improv'. It also starts a three-part series called 'Around the World', which has been an absolute highlight for most teachers.

Please note that for Lessons 6 to 10, only a short outline is provided herein. For access to the full lesson plans and videos of me demonstrating, head to nobookbeginners.com.

Objectives

- ♩ Work towards getting 'Thunder Showers' hands together.
- ♩ Add harmony to 'Rocky Mountain', and continue singing and playing by ear.
- ♩ Show students how they can use words to create rhythm to make music.
- ♩ Explore improvising by using motifs that sound like different parts of the world.
- ♩ Create a musical 'passport' for the 'Around the World Improv' to track their compositions and explorations.

Lesson 7

Students continue with another rote piece, improvising, harmony and the next section of the 'Around the World Improv'.

Objectives

- ♪ Expand the student's curiosity and sense of exploration through the 'Thunder Showers' improv.
- ♪ Continue refining singing and playing harmony.
- ♪ Review call-and-response work.
- ♪ Continue to enjoy the 'Around the World' improv and the sounds that different scales create.

Lesson 8

Students continue with 'Around the World', moving to a different country. They also learn a fun and familiar piece, something like 'The Simpsons Theme', and they do some more improvising.

Objectives

- ♪ You are almost purely improvising with the student now, so the objective is to engage and encourage their creativity through improvisation.

Lesson 9

Lesson 9 revisits the 'Breakfast Improv'. The student also does 'The Storm Improvisation' and finishes up the travels 'Around the World'.

Objectives

- ♪ Students continue having fun exploring the sounds of other countries and are introduced to the whole-tone ('alien') scale.
- ♪ Give students a taste of the blues with a slight change to the 'Breakfast Improv'.
- ♪ If you need more activities, you can start introducing your student to the 12-bar blues.

Lesson 10

Lesson 10 is a wrap-up, which includes an improvisation and mini concert.

Objectives

- ♪ Summarise the last ten weeks' work to show your student how far they've come.
- ♪ Give the student a chance for a mini performance of all they've achieved.
- ♪ Finish their 'Around the World' journey.

♪ If the student has learnt any other pieces along the way ('The Simpsons Theme', pop songs by ear, 'Chopsticks' etc.), allow them the opportunity to play through them during this lesson for their parents.

Beyond Lesson 10

From here, you can do whatever you wish! After working through ten weeks of NBB, you'll have no shortage of your own ideas for creativity!

And if you don't want to do Lessons 5 through 9, you can skip them or maybe just do the 'Around the World' improv for one or two weeks. That's totally fine. The great thing about the NBB framework is it's 100% flexible, so you can use it exactly how you want to.

The NBB Benefits

If you've come this far in the book, you have a solid understanding of why creativity is important and why reading can wait until you're at least a month into lessons. You now also have NBB lessons to try with your beginner students.

It can be overwhelming to think of changing the way you teach and that feeling can quickly see us revert to what we know best — the old approaches. I hate seeing that get in the way of meaningful change. If you are feeling overwhelmed, I urge you to take things slowly and operate at your own pace. The easiest way to do that is … just do one thing! Take *just one* of the ideas presented and start with that. It could be trying out Lesson 1 with *one* beginner student, perhaps the next one to enrol. Or it could be trying out *one* of the singing activities, games or improvisations with *one* student in *one* lesson. If you commit to trying *just one* thing, it will feel less overwhelming and you'll have a far better chance of success.

Think of what teachers often suggest to students who are struggling to get started with practice: 'Just sit at the piano and play your favourite piece. That's all!' Just being at their instrument will increase their chances of playing (practising) a little more by a significant margin.

Similarly, once you take that first step, you'll be on your way to enjoying all the NBB benefits, which are described in the following sections.

Increased Confidence in Yourself

You'll grow so much in confidence as you embark on your NBB journey. While the start of the process will take some preparation and might be a little nerve-wracking, all the teachers who've converted to this approach have never looked back. If you ever felt like your teaching was getting a little stale or you just needed to refresh yourself, this is the approach to try. Young teacher Edina describes her experience with NBB:

> *As a new piano teacher, NBB has helped guide me in teaching young beginners. I don't have any pedagogy training in piano, but I've been playing since I was eight. The students I have are the children of acquaintances. NBB was the first time I heard about learning without a book, and it's a wonderful, progressive method for which I've already received positive feedback from my parents.*

One of my favourite stories is how the NBB approach helped TopMusic member Alyssa move into full-time music teaching:

> *I just wanted to say a quick thank you. The NBB method is something I use with all my new*

students. I love the curriculum and so do my students. You are partially to thank for my decision to take the leap to quit my desk job and become a piano teacher. It was one of the best decisions I've ever made.

Students with Better Ears

I can't tell you the number of times I've taken on transfer students who are unable to sing back a tone played on the piano or to even sing a note and find it on the piano. Some also struggle to keep a steady beat, tap back a rhythm or sing at all. These are all things that change when you start working on musicality before reading with your beginner students. They will start to sing in tune. They'll be able to recognise cadences and harmony. They'll be able to sing intervals. And they'll enjoy it too!

Student Confidence

Ultimately, we want to give our students self-confidence by sowing the seed towards an identity as a musician when they're a little older.

One of the most challenging age groups for teachers is around ages 13–15 when many students quit music lessons. One of the factors that most supports students sticking with music long-term is if they *identify as a musician*. One of the best ways to build this is to give students the confidence to play in front of their friends, particularly to be able to play by ear and/or play popular music that everyone knows and loves. This is when our students start realising their friends think of them as the 'cool pianist who can play that Coldplay song', which reinforces to our students that, indeed, 'I'm a musician, so why would I quit now?'

As well-known composer, author and clinician Carol Matz shared with me on Episode 89 of the TopMusic Podcast, music was critical in her self-identity and esteem as a teenager:

> *I remember when I was in middle school … We were on a school trip and we were in an auditorium that had a piano. So I went over and started playing all the new Billy Joel songs. The other kids were hanging around, and they were singing, and it honestly just made me feel really cool and accepted. I was that girl who's 'good on the piano'. It was a big part of my identity and helped build my self-esteem. I really think the most important thing that a teacher can do is help students build their self-esteem. I always think that if my students take away nothing more than feeling good about themselves — who they are,*

what they can accomplish – then I helped them work on something that's going to change their lives in every aspect. We know that not every student is going to be a concert pianist or a jazz pianist playing gigs. But just having that ability to play the piano for a few friends or family members could really do a lot for a kid's sense of self-worth.

Starting your students with NBB is a great way to build self-confidence and begin the process towards musical identity as they get older.

Eagerness to Start Reading

It might sound counterintuitive, but I find that reading becomes a natural flow-on effect of the NBB lessons. It's much easier to transition to reading when the musical basics have already been explored.

Marketing

Another great benefit of NBB is that your creative approach will set you apart from other teachers and become a point of difference for you, which can be used in any traditional marketing you do. It will also help you grow your clientele via word of mouth. This can be particularly useful if you're operating in an area that has many teachers and thus a lot of competition.

Higher Retention

The immersive nature of NBB lessons will naturally lead to excitement and motivation for students and keep them coming back for more.

Happy Students

As you've no doubt realised from all the NBB teacher feedback you've read throughout this book, kids just *love it*! Kids get to be imaginative. They are invited to have fun, explore and create their own music. What's not to love?

Happy Parents

I've lost count of the amount of positive feedback NBB teachers have had from parents, most of whom will have had traditional lessons themselves. The parent's comments that piano teacher Kathryn mentions here are expressed in one way or another to many NBB teachers:

> *Taught a first lesson to a new student yesterday, and her mum said, 'Wow! How did you learn to teach piano like this? Is this how you were taught? Because it sure isn't how we were taught as kids.'*

The added benefit of this is that parents talk with other parents and your word-of-mouth marketing will buzz with creativity and send more students your way. Georgina had this to say:

> *Children are coming home really happy, telling their parents what fun they had in piano lessons and are immediately able to show them what they can do. Parents are happy. They can see their child is enjoying and learning, so it's a win-win. As a teacher, it's all great fun to use.*

Happy Teachers

Here's some more feedback collected from teachers over the years:

> *Have finished two lessons with a nine-year-old boy beginner. He is having so much fun not using books! Although tentative at first about improvising, he is now starting to listen more closely to the recording I made to get a feel for what he would like to play, which is encouraging. NBB has made a huge difference to the way I approach beginners — and some not so beginners too! Just wish I had found this fantastic resource sooner.*
> *– Lisa*

> *I had my first NBB lesson yesterday. I was terrified! But everything just flowed. Amazing!*

I am now rethinking every student's lesson to incorporate all I've learnt so far. This week has been very different around my studio and the kids love it! 'Frog and Snake' — so simple but so entertaining. Great stuff! Looking forward to learning even more!
– Lisa

I wanted to tell you about the six-year-old student I started using the NBB framework with. It basically saved this student. His mum was ready to drop lessons because what I was doing just wasn't working for him. He just absolutely loves the NBB lessons and I love teaching them. We started exploring the Egypt pentatonic scale this week. I made a passport for him and took a picture of him wearing an Egyptian headdress that he'd actually made.
– Rebecca

Thank you for all these wonderful ideas and resources! I've tried some out on my students already, and I'm surprised at how comfortable I am teaching through improv/rote without a method book. Your course has given me such clear ideas and guidelines. I'm bonding differently with my students too. That was a surprise bonus!
– Pinky

TAKEAWAYS

- ♪ NBB is primarily designed for beginners aged six to ten.

- ♪ While it is designed for the piano, the approach can be adapted for other instruments and groups.

- ♪ The core fundamentals of the program are exploration, creativity and fun; storytelling; a focus on only the most important technique basics, rather than all aspects of technique; an emphasis on the social side of music; and normalising singing.

- ♪ Don't let the thought of teaching piano differently overwhelm you. Start with just one thing — one lesson, one student, one activity — and build from there.

- ♪ The NBB benefits are many. Taking the time to explore this creative approach leads to important payoffs: increased confidence in yourself and your teaching, increased confidence in your students, students with better ears and students who are eager to start reading.

- ♪ Happy students plus happy parents equals higher retention, good marketing and, most importantly, an increased chance of producing lifelong musicians.

PART 4
Atypical Beginners

Not all beginner piano students fall in the six-to-ten age range that NBB is primarily designed for. This section addresses how NBB can be adapted to suit 'atypical beginners':

- ♪ preschoolers
- ♪ teens and adults
- ♪ transfer students
- ♪ students with additional needs.

Preschoolers

Back in 2018, I was lucky enough to have the amazing Irish teacher Nicola Cantan offer to create a version of NBB geared towards preschool students aged five and under, simply called 'Preschool NBB'. Nicola came with an absolute wealth of experience working with younger students and was already well known as our TopMusicPro Community Manager. So, I was only too happy for her to be involved, especially given my own very limited experience teaching music to this age group. And the results speak for themselves! As one of our members, Jimmi, said:

> *Preschool-/kindergarten-age students are a breed unto themselves … and breaking down the elements has been a game changer for me to reach little ones and has created more personal teaching creativity to complement this course as well.*

The Preschool NBB course, which is available inside TopMusicPro Membership[23], is broken down in a similar way to the regular NBB course. Over the span of ten lessons, which might take ten weeks or more, you'll get step-by-step instructions and lesson plans for exactly what to do with your preschool students. And because it was created by a master of piano teaching games (Nicola), you know it's going to be super fun and packed with engaging activities perfectly suited to this age group!

Here's what Beth told us about her Preschool NBB experience:

> *I have taught piano for 35-plus years, changed my teaching philosophy umpteen times, switched*

> *favourite curriculums at least half a dozen times and constantly struggled to introduce piano concepts to the youngest students, with the currently available curriculum. They always assumed too much understanding of musical concepts, coordination, parental knowledge, student self-control etc. and rely way too much on students being able to 'read' or at least 'track' from left to right in their materials. I just started my third preschooler today using Preschool NBB. He loved his first lesson, even though he was apprehensive at first. So. Much. Fun!*

And here's more praise for the Preschool NBB course from Selena:

> *I started lessons with the three-year-old sibling of one of my current students last week. I searched for and found the fabulous resource Preschool NBB and totally used the lesson plan for the first lesson! It was a huge success and I loved having fresh ideas for an age group that usually intimidates me as a teacher.*

If you haven't taught preschoolers before, you're in for a treat but also a bit of a learning curve. Here are some important considerations for teachers new to this age group.

Keyboard Geography

You're going to have to slow down and break down concepts that you're only used to briefly mentioning to older students. One of the big skills taught throughout the ten weeks is keyboard geography and navigation. Preschoolers won't yet have the pattern-recognition skills that make this obvious to older children and adults.

Aural Skills

A huge benefit of the NBB approach is that you can get your students to switch on their ears right from the start. This is doubly true for preschoolers. By focusing on listening and experiencing pitches and rhythms, preschool piano students can get a massive head start that will serve them for the rest of their lives. The preschool students who stay with you in the long term will be some of your most intuitively musical students if you tap into this in the first lessons.

Technique and Posture

One of the mistakes many teachers make when first teaching young beginners is to expect them to play in a five-finger position. This is not only something you will need to build up to over time but is not even desirable in the beginning stages. We want our students to learn to play with arm weight and use their bodies at the piano with ease, which is better achieved through playing non-legato and using the strongest fingers for at least the first few lessons.

You will need to have adaptations in place so that your preschool students can sit comfortably at the piano. Make sure you have something to raise the bench to the appropriate height and something for them to plant their feet on. If you do not have an adjustable bench, you can use carpet squares or play mats stacked on top of each other to raise the height. Just make sure they are stable and steady. Preschoolers are prone to wiggling around!

If you can get your hands on a pedal extender, it's fantastic to have one in place for your young students so they can explore all the sounds of the piano. If that's not possible, a simple footstool or box will do nicely. Make sure that it is high enough. Bathroom footstools that you can buy for children to reach the sink are usually too low, especially for three- and four-year-olds.

Parent Involvement

The younger the student, the bigger the role the parent needs to take in their practice and progress at the piano. Make sure to be clear about this from the very beginning and let the parent know that their role is vital to their child's success.

If possible, I advise having the parent sit in on the lessons, at least for the first few if not beyond. Spend the last few minutes of the lesson reviewing with the parent what needs to be practised. If they cannot make it to the lesson in person, send them videos or detailed instructions via email so that they can get involved at home.

If you are a bit hesitant to take on preschoolers, take some inspiration from Lasia:

> *Just wanted to share that I started a new student on the Preschool NBB method and it's great! I had previously lost a seven-year-old boy because lessons weren't 'fun enough'. So his mum just figured he wasn't ready to take lessons right now. He has a low attention span and doesn't like to stay on the bench very long. I started him off using a method book and quickly realised what a mistake that was!*
>
> *He isn't exactly mature enough for the regular NBB course, so I decided that even though Preschool NBB is designed for preschoolers, I would try it anyway. So far, he loves it, and I don't think that's going to change.*

I encourage anyone hesitant to include preschoolers in your studio to step outside of your comfort zone and just do it! I believe they are a fun part of piano teaching and they will literally keep you on your toes!

By the way, don't worry if you don't get everything right straight off. Try to embark on all this with the same attitude a preschooler would — with a sense of play and exploration!

Teens and Adults

As students grow older, we need different strategies and activities to engage them. Teens and adults need lots of autonomy and a clear path to achieving their own musical goals.

Firstly, it's important to know that, in its current form, the content of the NBB lesson plans will not be suitable for teens or adults. The underlying principles of the framework are sound for beginners of all ages:

- ♪ playing by ear
- ♪ improvising
- ♪ singing
- ♪ learning rote pieces
- ♪ playing chords and harmony
- ♪ keeping a steady beat and tapping rhythms.

But the activities in the NBB framework are devised specifically to suit younger children and will not resonate with teens, who will quickly find them childish and embarrassing.

What should we do instead? While it's beyond the scope of this book to go into too much detail, here are a few thoughts about beginner teens and adults (two groups I tend to bundle together).

Firstly, find out what they want to learn and why they're starting piano lessons. This is critical. You'll need to help them achieve this goal, whatever it is, through the course of your instruction. Secondly, start working on some music that is familiar to them — a pop song, a classical favourite. Whatever it is, this will give them an instant buzz and excitement to continue. Thirdly, I take all my teens and adults through a simple instruction in chord playing, based around a framework I've created called '4 Chord Composing'. You can find out more about how to use this yourself at topmusic.co/chords.

I always start with chords because for most adults, especially those who've learnt as a child, it's literally mind-blowing for them to realise they can play familiar and impressive-sounding music using just a few chords. If they learnt classically as a child, they might never have been exposed to chords and harmony and therefore have a very narrow experience of music, but with TopMusic resources, you can change this and open their eyes to the joys of music creativity through chord playing and improvisation.

I recommend starting with at least four to five 'no book' lessons, focusing on teaching them songs they enjoy (you can do this through chords and/or by rote) and exploring chord-based playing before introducing reading (if that's something they even want to learn!). Keep things light, flexible, positive and fun so they keep motivated and excited to learn more.

Transfer Students

When we start a new transfer student, it can be hard to know even where to begin. The great news is that, since you're reading this book, it's likely that you're going to bring a much better musical experience than the student has encountered before, and therefore you won't have to do anything particularly amazing to have a big impact on them.

More often than not, when I take a transfer teenager through my chord-teaching approach, they are speechless and wonder why on earth they were never exposed to this in the years they were studying with their other teacher. I shrug and tell them that I'm doing my best to change this!

Transfer students come with so many potential strengths and weaknesses. You first need to diagnose where they're at. I do this through the 'Transfer Student Diagnostic' that comes with my course about teaching teens called *Teen and Transfer Student Teaching Toolkit* (yes, I enjoy alliteration), available to members of TopMusicPro. This diagnostic is a checklist you can go through with any new student so that you can feel confident of where they are strong and where you'll need to help them.

Like teens and adults, transfer students of any age will appreciate a discussion about their goals and the music they like to play and will enjoy you helping them with that alongside the skills they need to develop over time. Once you know where they're at, you can start setting a plan for their development. Regardless of whether they are readers or not, I'd still advocate a NBB approach for the first few lessons. This will not only allow you to confirm your initial diagnosis of their ability but also give you both a chance to get to know each other and settle on your plan of action for the coming year.

Neurodiverse Students and those with Exceptionalities

Perhaps you notice that a trusted approach isn't quite working for one of your students, that distractions are sidetracking progress, or even that you're feeling not so confident with enquiries that begin with 'My child has exceptionalities but would enjoy music study. Are you well prepared to teach them?'

ATYPICAL BEGINNERS

Working with students with exceptionalities can be a very rewarding experience. By understanding our students' needs better and adapting our music-learning environment, we can offer a tailored learning experience — and feel more confident saying yes to music teaching for these amazing students.

Rita has this to say:

> *My two neurodiverse students are responding really well to the many 'off-bench' activities from NBB. 'Thunder Showers' is proving to be a wonderful way for them to play something significant very early on — they love this piece. 'Frog and Snake' is a fabulous game I'm using to teach all my beginners the notes on the keys, so this is well on the way to security by the time we meet notes in print. Last week I played what I call 'Drop Down' with a couple of young students: I dropped their fingers onto the keys, and they figured out how to play 'Merrily We Roll Along' wherever they land. I love this!*

Andrew and Joanne left this comment on one of my YouTube videos explaining that not worrying about reading is perfect for vision-impaired students:

> *Love this because I am doing some very basic introductory lessons with blind kids. Fabulous ideas as we cannot use books!*

Susan used NBB for a student with Asperger syndrome:

> *Today was a first lesson for a young student with Asperger's and it was the perfect way to get him started and engaged. He wasn't overwhelmed and didn't feel he had to stick to the exact page in a book. We created music together and explored the keyboard. I find your resources have really changed the way I think about teaching piano.*

One of our lovely TopMusicPro members, Selena Pistoresi, created a complete online course about teaching neurodiverse students in our academy a few years ago. (The course is still available for members.) Selena notes that neurodiverse students often resonate better with fewer choices. For example, use only a small range of keys on the piano (unlike some of the NBB improvisation activities that move all over the piano) and NBB will likely need to be adapted to suit students with varying abilities. She said:

> *I totally agree that students should get comfortable as early as possible moving all over the keyboard and not being married to any position. But students who have poor motor skills, especially fine motor skills, often can't initiate movements on their own or make purposeful movements.*

ATYPICAL BEGINNERS

Some students can't even hover their hand over the piano if you ask them to. So I think it's really important to start in a single five-finger position; I use C position in the beginning so they can start to develop keyboard awareness.

There's still that component of 'Here's C, then D, E, F, G'. But for now, your thumb is always your C finger, finger two is always your D finger ... just so that they have something to anchor them right in the beginning. And they're still playing songs that are fairly interesting. Five keys are better than the normal two or three black keys and typical at the prereading stage.

But that way, it just kind of draws them in, and they'll have time to build their motor skills and keyboard awareness first. And then, of course, you can always branch out to other positions.

Ultimately, success with this group will depend on your diagnosis of their ability in their first lesson, discussions with their parents and constant adjustment and refinement.

TAKEAWAYS

♪ Teaching beginner piano to preschoolers can be a daunting thought. Nicola Cantan has created a version of NBB geared towards preschoolers that has been well received in the TopMusic community.

♪ The specific NBB activities are not suitable for teens or adults as this group of students will find them childish and embarrassing, but you can still take a 'no book' approach with this group. Focus on teaching them songs they enjoy and explore chord-based playing before introducing reading (if that's something they want to learn).

♪ When you take on a transfer student, it's a good idea to establish their strengths and weaknesses before commencing teaching them. I've developed a diagnostic tool for this purpose, which is available to TopMusicPro members.

♪ Teaching neurodiverse students and those with exceptionalities can be very rewarding, and many of the NBB activities are suitable for these students.

Conclusion

Few teachers get the opportunity to affect lives as deeply as music teachers do. Few teachers get to work one-on-one with students over the span of a decade or more. Few teachers know their students' parents and family lives as well as you do.

You are not a babysitter. Yours isn't a hobby career. You aren't merely an instructor or tutor. Your work is your life's passion. You are a professional educator. You've worked for years to be able to do what you do. In fact, you probably started building these skills well before you were ten. What other career path begins while your age is still in the single digits?!

You undertake professional development and attend conferences. You've taken the time to attain qualifications. You have experience and passion in spades.

You've chosen this career because you believe in the future. You believe in young people. You believe in the power of music to change lives. It's not about money, fame or glamour. A heart-led decision brought you here and I'm so grateful you've made this decision to change lives.

You're also *more* than 'just a teacher' in so many ways. You're the counsellor, the wise friend, the confidant, the trusted adult to whom students can turn. You see all sides of them. They can take off their masks and let down their guard because of the trust you've cultivated over many years. You matter more than you can imagine in the lives of your students.

* * *

A shift to a more creative approach in piano teaching has been happening for around ten years, and it's been so exciting to see how many teachers have been embracing creativity. My hope in writing this book is that it will help to slowly phase out the 'old school' approach (and the methods that go with it) over time. Just by reading this book, you have become part of that movement. I'm confident you're excited by the possibilities and eager to get started.

So don't let me keep you any longer. Let me send you on your way with some words from the manifesto I created

CONCLUSION

for the TopMusicPro community, which helps to explain who we are and what we stand for. After reading this book, I hope these words will resonate with you too.

> TopMusicTeachers do things differently.
>
> We no longer teach the way we were taught.
>
> We create unique learning experiences for every student.
>
> We have a student-centred approach to teaching.
>
> Our approach is integrated, bringing together reading and performance with creativity, curiosity and exploration.
>
> We believe in helping students find connections to deepen understanding.
>
> We ask more and tell less.
>
> We know the world is changing faster than ever and we're committed to continuous learning.
>
> We don't give up on difficult students and we open our doors to diversity.
>
> We don't teach reading in Lesson one.
>
> Pop songs don't scare us.
>
> YouTube is our friend.
>
> Music teaching is more than a hobby.

We are CEOs of our studios.

We know our business and charge what we are worth.

We are 'open door' teachers; we thrive on brainstorming solutions and sharing our resources with other teachers.

Together, we change lives and bring more music into the world.

We are TopMusicTeachers.

Epilogue

I've just returned from the 2023 National Conference on Keyboard Pedagogy (NCKP), the first in-person music conference I've attended in four years, and I've been reminiscing about how much has changed in the world of piano pedagogy since I first attended the conference and spoke back in 2015. As you'll remember from the introduction to this book, it was the 2015 conference where I first heard about Music Learning Theory (MLT) and where I gave my first talk in America on teaching pop music.

I'm delighted to say *so* much has changed! Back in 2015, there were very few (if any) other presentations at NCKP on teaching pop styles. In fact, there were probably only two or three other sessions on general creativity over the entire four days. And this was mirrored more broadly in the wider community. There were few blogs sharing creative teaching ideas at the time, even fewer podcasts and a dearth of resources and training courses for teachers to explore and buy online.

Fast forward eight years to 2023. Not only can attendees at NCKP enjoy creative-teaching sessions galore but there are whole 'creative tracks' (or streams through the conference) and even creativity committees. And there are now literally hundreds of teachers selling creative resources online; multiple training courses from individuals and institutions; well over 25 podcasts focused on piano pedagogy, business and creativity; and thousands of resources, articles, blogs and videos. How times have changed! When once the conference speakers driving creative change were indulged with a raised eyebrow or two, I feel we are now embraced and even championed.

I give credit to NCKP and its organisers for the leadership and growth it has shown in this area. And kudos to all the teachers of the world who are now sharing their resources and expertise so freely. The saying 'A high tide lifts all boats' has never been more apt! Indeed, it's been heartwarming to see how both teachers and organisations alike have accepted the power of teaching outside the box and how a more flexible and student-centred approach can have an outsized impact on our students.

EPILOGUE

Still, we have a long way to go!

There are many thousands of teachers around the world who aren't able to attend conferences but for whom the ideas in this book will make a world of difference to their teaching. There are teachers who are unaware of the educational research driving changes in music pedagogy and how much their students could benefit from a fresh perspective.

There are many teachers continuing to teach the way they were taught, using the same methods and approaches they experienced as children, whose students are missing out on a world of exploration, enquiry and a deeper connection with their innate musicality.

My hope in writing this book is that teachers will reconsider their approach; seek out further education and mentorship; aim to continually reassess, reinvent and redesign themselves; and explore lessons that put students at the heart of their own music-learning experience.

If you know a teacher who could benefit from this book, please tell them about it. If you're a parent of a music student who can see gaps in your child's education, please let their teacher know about us.

***

I had the pleasure of interviewing Mike Grande this morning for my podcast. Mike has been a friend of mine for many years and runs three hugely successful music schools in New York and Florida. He's an incredible educator and entrepreneur, and I always finish our conversations buzzing with ideas and considering the bigger picture about what we do as teachers.

As we were wrapping up our conversation, we turned to his schools' mission. If there is one extra thing that I encourage teachers to contemplate as they finish reading this book, it's this: What is the real, deep, underlying purpose to your teaching? What is your mission?

As Mike said during our interview, 'You're not teaching every single person that walks into your music studio to be a concert musician or rock star. Students want to play an instrument because they just love music. So it's about what else they're getting out of it'. The mission of Mike's *Rock Out Loud* music schools is all about students developing life skills and getting their confidence and self-esteem to a level they've never seen before.

What's your teaching really about? What are you trying to develop in your students each week in your studio? If you give yourself time to think, you'll realise that your purpose is about much more than reading or performance. It's about life.

Tim Topham
Melbourne, August 2023

Resources

THE TOPMUSICPRO COMMUNITY

I was lucky when I started teaching piano because I had a mentor. I had reconnected by chance with my childhood piano teacher, Miss Mac, and began an apprenticeship of sorts. I worked together with her and, over the course of two or three years, learnt everything I could about piano teaching.

Soon after reconnecting with Miss Mac around 2008 when I was 30.

Having not gone to a conservatory, I didn't start with any preconceived ideas of how music teaching should work. I tested an approach, and if I didn't like it, I tried something new. I challenged assumptions, asked lots of questions and slowly gained confidence as I saw my students thrive. But I realise that not everyone is as confident experimenting in lessons as I am, not everyone has had formal training and not everyone is lucky enough to have had someone mentor and nurture them.

In my experience, most teachers like step-by-step plans for how to teach something if it's outside their comfort zone. They enjoy downloads and cheat sheets that help guide them along the way. They are open to experimenting but within a safe structure. They want to be able to ask questions, watch teaching videos and know that they're on the right track.

So how *do* you find support when you're stuck in your studio all day? How do you connect with other people, test new ideas and hold yourself accountable for change? Well, that's *exactly* why I created TopMusicPro — the kind of community that I would have loved to have been a part of when I started teaching and one that you can become a part of today.

TopMusicPro is a community of dedicated, hardworking and vibrant teachers committed to not only creating the best experiences and outcomes for their students but also ensuring their own lifestyle is both secure and

RESOURCES

sustainable. No matter what stage of teaching you're at, or what training you have (if any), or how many students you teach, or where you are in the world, or what you think about pedalling in the music of Bach, TopMusicPro is a place where everyone can share, question, challenge and contribute in a safe and supportive environment. If you are struggling, lacking a bit of confidence, feeling isolated and a bit flat in your teaching unsure of how to move forward, or just needing confirmation that you're on the right track, then you are *exactly* the right person for TopMusicPro.

I invite you to allow me to continue to support your teaching journey through our global community of music teachers, particularly if you are looking to do the following:

- ♪ Find ways to prepare students for *their future* instead of *our past*.
- ♪ Gain confidence in running your studio business.
- ♪ Work more creatively with students.
- ♪ Boost your studio numbers.
- ♪ Teach difficult students more effectively.
- ♪ Integrate music theory and practice more deeply.

If you're interested in joining, you can find out more at topmusicpro.com.

Remember to get this!

If you have not done so already, make sure you visit our companion website at nobookbeginners.com, where you can watch videos of me teaching the NBB approach, download complete lesson plans for Lessons 1 - 5 of the framework and access all associated resources including backing tracks, sheet music, practice plans and much more.

DOWNLOAD NOW!

nobookbeginners.com

Social Media Links

Facebook

facebook.com/groups/topmusic.co

Follow our page. We'd love to welcome you to the official TopMusic Facebook group: 'Piano Teachers with Beginner and Intermediate Students.'

YouTube

youtube.com/@topmusicco

Instagram

instagram.com/topmusic.co

TikTok

tiktok.com/@topmusic.co

20 Creative Ways to Start a Piano Lesson

Here are 20 ideas to get your creative juices flowing! If you'd like to download this with links to resources, head to the nobookbeginners.com resources section. You can also see me teaching these at the piano if you visit my TikTok channel, tiktok.com/@topmusic.co.

1. Using a notated piece the student is learning, have them create an intro or coda in the style of the piece.

2. Download the MusiClock app and use it as a backing track for scales.

3. Get off the bench and play some games. There are hundreds of sites sharing musical games for piano teachers. Just search online.

4. Explore rhythms using percussion activities on buckets or with plastic cups. Both are total winners and will have you and your student laughing in no time.

5. Instead of just playing a scale over MusiClock or another backing track, have the student improvise something using the notes of the scale.

6. Play from lead sheets. Search online for 'piano lead sheets' to find heaps of options — hymns, folk tunes, jazz and so on. The lead sheet collection *101 Classical Themes for Buskers* is also an awesome resource for this.

7. Explore the 12 bar blues. You can find free lesson plans at topmusic.co/blues.

8. Play a musical game on an iPad. Check my list of the 'Best iPad apps for Piano Teachers' at topmusic.co/ipad.

9. Teach the 'Four Chord Song' — the chord progression I–V–vi–IV in any key — and get your students grooving along to a pop song that uses it. (There are hundreds.)

10. Ask a student what they'd like to learn, find the music and help them with it. Be prepared to help with anything and be prepared to simplify creatively! See the *Pop Song Solutions* member videos for how I teach lots of current pop songs — available inside TopMusicPro.

11. Ask your student if they've recently tried learning something from a YouTube tutorial or encourage them to do so if they haven't, then have them show you what they've learnt.

20 CREATIVE WAYS TO START A PIANO LESSON

12. Add all your students' scales to the Decide Now! app so students can spin the wheel to choose their scale and/or way of playing it.

13. For your student's next reading piece, pull apart the patterns in the music and explore these ingredients before they start learning the notes. Find out more about this approach at topmusic.co/patterns.

14. Teach the student a pop song riff by rote. You can find them in my 'Top 10 Pop Songs for Piano Students' blog at topmusic.co/pop.

15. For young students, ask them to make up a piece that tells a story about animals — 'The Ant versus the Elephant', 'The Bees Attack!', or 'Mice Marching'. Great for beginners, this is one of the first activities in the NBB framework.

16. Try musical echoes/chants: You play something on the piano and the student copies you, keeping a steady beat (and not missing a beat) and watching what you do. Keep it at the right level depending on your student.

17. As a variation of idea 16, the student copies you but without seeing what you play. They have to listen and copy back in time by using just their ears. Kids love the challenge! Then, have them play something and you echo it back to them. Get creative!

18. Work out a tune together by ear with no music. This could be classical, pop, anything. Something they choose and know is best. Get them to sing the melodies before they try to play them. (Success is unlikely otherwise!)

19. Teach the chords for 'Heart and Soul' (a I–vi–IV–V chord progression) in C major and improvise over it.

20. Go to hooktheory.com/trends, where students can click the chords in a progression and hear all the songs that use that progression. Get them to play the progression they choose on the piano while the song plays.

Acknowledgements

Very rarely is a book solely the creation of one person, and this book is no exception. Many teachers, colleagues, family members and friends have contributed to the ideas presented, shared stories with me, tested the self-assessments and read manuscripts, drafts, and final proofs.

Huge thanks and gratitude go out to:

- ♪ My amazing team at topmusic.co — Mauro, Sara, Ruth, Jill, Tara, Timz, Georgina, Albert, Ruby, Tudor, Cristian, David, Kimberly, Rebecca and Michael — many of whom contributed feedback during the writing process.

- ♪ Members of my team who helped test out the self-assessments and provided advice on many aspects of the book: in particular Rebecca Stewart, Rosemarie Penner, Anamarie

Sabbagh, Tara Wright, Georgina Wilson and Janna Williamson. A special thanks to each of them.

♪ To my TopMusicPro members, past and present — you've been the teachers who have allowed me to create so many resources and share them with the world. Thank you for contributing your stories and ideas to our community and supporting me as I've built the business over the years.

♪ Our blog readers, podcast listeners (some of whom have been with us since Episode 1!), YouTube watchers and all our friends on social media. Thanks for your comments and suggestions. I can't tell you how much easier it is to host a live video when people are contributing.

♪ All my podcast interviewees (over 300 and counting) and all the teachers who've co-hosted webinars and workshops with me over the years — thanks for sharing your ideas so freely.

♪ All the teachers quoted in the book. Thanks for sharing your stories. I hope the NBB approach is continuing to provide you and your students with joy.

ACKNOWLEDGEMENTS

- ♪ To my hubby David for supporting me on this journey of creating TopMusic over more than a decade and for going 'all-in' with me when I decided to pursue TopMusic full-time in 2017.

- ♪ Mr Trevor Henley, Director of Music at Camberwell Grammar, where I attended high school — your mentoring and friendship fanned the flames of a lifetime of music.

- ♪ Family friend Richard Strachan ('Strachs') — you gave a young Tim a tape called *Tim's Tape* in 1988 and followed it up at regular intervals (eventually graduating to CD!) with new collections featuring a mix of classical music that I still listen to today. You'll sadly never know the impact you had on my musical formation but I'll be forever grateful for the compilations and notes you put together.

- ♪ My structural editor and designer Kelly Exeter who was able to massage my initial writing into much clearer sections and provide project management and advice every step of the way.

- ♪ Last but definitely not least, my line and copy editor and music engraver (and also our amazing TopMusicCo publishing coordinator) Albert Mendoza who turned this manuscript into something more flowing, smooth, perfect and professional than I could ever have imagined. Thank you, Albert — this book would not be the same quality without your incredible care and attention.

I would also like to remember Forrest Kinney, our dear friend and fellow creative-teaching maestro, who gave so much to the world of creative piano pedagogy. While you'll be sorely missed for years to come, your legacy lives on.

Long overdue are thanks to my parents, Richard and Jill, for taking me to piano lessons as a chubby eight-year-old and to my Godmother, Jenny Gillies, for referring us to Miss Mac for lessons.

***

Now, this might be the first time that I've admitted this publicly, but at times I was a pretty bad piano student! My parents remind me of how infuriated and embarrassed they got when I refused to perform when they asked me to and how I once ran and hid at a recital to avoid having to play. I could be a bolshy, stubborn kid, but my parents and Miss Mac stood by me, taught me the music I wanted to learn and never lost sight of the musician I could become. I can't thank them enough.

Soon after I took my Grade 6 exam at age 12, Miss Mac realised that my heart wasn't in classical music, so she

ACKNOWLEDGEMENTS

introduced me to legendary jazz pianist Steve Sedergreen, who took me under his wing and taught me much about chords, comping and improvising for the next couple of years.

Glenn Riddle reluctantly took me through Victorian Certificate of Education (VCE) Music Performance at Camberwell Grammar School on piano, but I think was infuriated by my disdain for anything classical and the fact that I just wanted to play ragtime and pop music. I much preferred playing the piano for the school musical productions anyway!

From then on, my musical life took a whole variety of twists and turns that I believe have directly influenced the teacher I am today and the advice I've been able to provide other teachers. I've worked as a classroom teacher for over 20 years. I've taught in primary and secondary schools in Australia and the UK. I've taught subjects as varied as maths, information technology, physical education, outdoor education and health and worked for many years as a substitute teacher in schools across Melbourne and Perth. TopMusic is really the culmination of all the teaching ideas that I've gathered from these experiences over the years. Thanks to everyone who's been a part of my journey.

About the Author

An internationally recognised leader in music education, Tim Topham has been helping to reshape and recharge the often-traditional landscape of instrumental music lessons.

Tim's vision of a more creative, modern and integrated approach to music teaching has seen him speak on stages from the US to the UK and Australia, publish numerous articles and record hundreds of podcasts and teaching videos for teachers.

In Tim's 20-plus-year international teaching career, he has been a classroom teacher, private studio teacher, head of department and head of campus, teaching and coordinating subjects including outdoor education, mathematics, information technology and, of course, music. He has held teaching posts at schools including Oundle School in the UK, Guildford Grammar School in Perth and Xavier College in Melbourne.

Tim's holistic approach to teaching music goes far beyond the traditional areas of technique, musicianship and performance of standard repertoire. His contemporary teaching strategies include improvising, playing chords, interpreting lead sheets, understanding pop music, playing by ear, using technology and engaging with music in a way that resonates with young people and inspires them to continue playing well into adulthood.

Tim is the author of *No Book Beginners*, a leading text demonstrating the many benefits of delaying reading in beginner piano teaching. Tim holds a Bachelor of Music, a Diploma of Education and a Master of Business Administration in Educational Leadership. He also holds a Diploma in Piano Performance (AMusA).

Tim is the founder of topmusic.co and, when he's not in the studio, enjoys cycling, coffee and travelling with his family.

Endnotes

1. Sam Holland, 'Update on Dr. Edwin Gordon's NCKP Keynote' in *Piano Inspires*, July 22, 2015, https://pianoinspires.com/update-on-dr-edwin-gordons-nckp-keynote/.

2. Paul Myatt, 'Why Teaching Music Reading Is the Wrong Way to Teach Piano [Part 1]', *Beginners* (blog), July 11, 2016, https://topmusic.co/why-teaching-music-reading-is-the-wrong-way-to-teach-piano-part-1/.

3. For one of the best demonstrations of MLT — and particularly one of its key tenets, audiation — check out topmusic.co/episode51.

4. I also tested Marilyn Lowe's *Music Moves for Piano* but found it very hard to understand and a leap too far from my own methods. So the books were never really used.

5   Exploring motive-based improvisations that speak to particular countries is a key part of the NBB lesson content from Lesson 6 and one that students absolutely adore.

6   Paul G. Woodford, 'Evaluating Edwin Gordon's Music Learning Theory from a Critical Thinking Perspective', *Philosophy of Music Education Review* 4/2 (Fall 1996), 83–95.

7   If you're new to TopMusicPro, it's our membership site for instrumental and vocal music teachers featuring training courses, lesson plans and teaching resources. You can learn more and join the fun at topmusicpro.com.

8   Lucinda Mackworth-Young, 'Why Every Study Should Know Happy Birthday with Lucinda Mackworth-Young', *Integrated Music Teaching Podcast*, Episode 110, October 27, 2017, https://topmusic.co/cptp110-why-every-student-should-know-happy-birthday-with-lucinda-mackworth-young/.

9   Seth Godin, excerpt from a speech given to a small class of Carnegie Mellon University final year music performance students. Original source unknown. Audio excerpt presented as part of my 'Entrepreneurial Musician' keynote for DAYTiME

conference series run by Music EDnet, 2016. Original audio available at 20m26s here: https://vimeo.com/topmusicco/sethgodin?ts=1226000.

10 Forrest Kinney, Music-Creativity-Joy: Exploring the Four Arts of Music (North Bend, WA: Two Streams Press, 2018), 74.

11 Seth Lorinczi, 'A Brief History of Music Publishing', Songtrust (blog), April 3, 2018, https://blog.songtrust.com/brief-history-of-the-music-publishing.

12 Forrest Kinney, Ibid.

13 Doreen Hall, 'Piano Methods: A Brief History' in *Paloma Piano* (blog), https://palomapiano.com/blog-post/piano-method-books-a-brief-history/.

14 Anya Wassenberg, 'The Piano Market Is Booming, and It's All Because of China', *Ludwig Van*, April 13, 2019, https://www.ludwig-van.com/toronto/2019/08/13/feature-the-piano-market-is-booming-and-its-all-because-of-china/.

15 For more about this approach, which I call 'Integrated Music Teaching', head to topmusic.co/integrated.

16 Martha Baker-Jordan, *Practical Piano Pedagogy* (Van Nuys, CA: Alfred Music, 2003), 353.

17 Elissa Milne, referenced in Why I Teach Beginner Piano Students Without a Method Book, blog post by Tim Topham, topmusic.co, 2017. https://topmusic.co/why-i-teach-beginner-piano-students-without-a-method-book/.

18 In this book, the words *parent, parents, guardian* and *guardians* are used interchangeably.

19 Teachers can purchase one of these by searching for 'ladybird toy' on Amazon or similar sites.

20 Dr Julie Knerr Hague, 'Mini Essay 5: Technique Basics for Beginners', pianosafari.com, https://pianosafari.com/wp-content/uploads/2016/04/Mini-Essay-5.pdf.

21 Tim Topham, 'Fun Piano Game for Beginner Music Students: Frog and Snake', video, August 20, 2018, https://www.youtube.com/watch?v=6dXodncH_XE.

22 'Audiation', The Gordon Institute for Music Learning (website), https://giml.org/mlt/audiation/.

23 topmusicpro.com

www.ingramcontent.com/pod-product-compliance
Lightning Source LLC
Chambersburg PA
CBHW062048290426
44109CB00027B/2766